Brotherhood of the Fin

A Coast Guard Rescue Swimmer's Story

GERALD R. HOOVER

Brotherhood of the Fin: A Coast Guard Rescue Swimmer's Story

Published by Wheatmark™
610 East Delano Street, Suite 104
Tucson, Arizona 85705 U.S.A.
www.wheatmark.com

ISBN-13: 978-1-58736-744-1
ISBN-10: 1-58736-744-0
Library of Congress Control Number: 2006940830

This book is dedicated to all the flight mechanics that kept me alive long enough to write it.
Thank You

Contents

Author's Note

The adventures you are about to read are real. They helped shape the history of Coast Guard and the lives of those we've touched. These stories began in 1983 on the night an old freighter sank, killing 31 of 34 men. A lot has happened to me since then and I tried to capture those events as accurately as possible. As with any endeavor that relies on human memory, the stories are not exact. I spent years tracking down the details, but have surely missed a few, or remembered them differently than someone else. Time may have colored the pictures in my mind, and these stories are limited to my perspective. If I failed to portray an event, individual, or dialog as someone else remembered it I ask for your understanding.

Inevitably some details are lost. Maybe it was a first name, a specific date, or an aircraft tail number. These facts were important and I exhausted all avenues of research before going ahead without those specifics. If you notice such a glaring oversight, just smile and keep reading.

Thank you for choosing to read my book.

CHAPTER 1

Bandit

The night of 18 January 1991, started like every other duty night but was quickly seared into my memory because of a 63-foot shrimp boat named *Bandit*. I came on duty at noon. My watch and that of my fellow Coasties would last for 24 hours. In the early afternoon we might go on a training flight or perform scheduled inspections of the helicopters—keeping our skills sharp while waiting to be called upon.

Late that afternoon the National Weather Service had issued a gale warning, and we could see from the low-slung clouds speeding by and shaking leaves on the trees that the report was true. The rain arrived later, creating a symphony of cymbals on the hangar's aluminum roof.

Like overprotective owners of fancy sports cars, we pamper our helicopters, knowing we must rely on them for our lives. We would surely do so that January day. Before the worst of the weather crossed our tarmac we put the HH-65 Dolphin helicopters in the safety of the large hangar, closing the giant garage door. While all 80 persons assigned to Air Station New Orleans must report to work each day, only a small number of us stay the night. On this night there were four enlisted men standing overnight duty: watch captain, flight mechanic, rescue swimmer, and line crewman.

Once the long day was done, we generally watched a movie, prepared dinner, or shot the breeze. Most air stations operate like fire departments, providing single beds known as racks in sleeping quarters for the crews. At Air Station New Orleans the bunkrooms were on the second deck over the hangar, with a kitchen and TV room downstairs. The quarters had recently been refurbished, so that they looked like simple hotel rooms and the only thing missing was room service. The small single beds, two to a room, provided little more than a place to lay our heads while we waited to be called. That night, in view of the heavy rain and stout winds, I remember thinking I should turn in early but the opportunity never came.

I had been standing duty for three years before the *Bandit* entered my life. My unit usually responded to 400 Search and Rescue (SAR) cases per year and each one I took part in transformed my helicopter into a classroom, the events becoming my teachers. Some cases became routine—mistaken flare sightings, prank calls and the like, but others called for true grit. The weather wasn't the only cause for search and rescue. Thirty thousand oilrig workers made a living offshore and we were often called on to be an ambulance service. On that particular January night, by the time the yellow tow tractor had rolled into the barn, I felt sure we would see some action. In fact, the events leading up to our launch were already beginning to take place just 50 miles away.

The captain of the *Bandit* was using the ship's wooden steering wheel to try and control the boat, whispering prayers as he struggled to keep his livelihood afloat. They were floundering in 15 foot seas created by 55-knot onshore winds. As they approached land, the waves piled close together, increasing the pounding effect. The *Bandit* reeled from it. The crew struggled to find protection behind an uninhabited barrier island about five miles off the Mississippi coast. These barrier islands are little more than sandbars with hearty, brushy growth of sea grapes and palm trees. The *Bandit* was heading for a cut of water known as Ship Island Pass, but more water was coming over the bow than the pumps could handle. The captain, John G. Crawford of Pearl River, Louisiana, broadcast a Mayday at about 7:50 PM.

The radio watch stander at Coast Guard Station Gulfport, Mississippi, received the distress call over the open airwaves of Channel 16, the international hailing and distress frequency. The Coast Guard's main means of rescue was a 41-foot aluminum-hulled boat, powered by twin turbo-charged Cummins diesel engines. These boats are identified by their hull numbers, the first two of which indicate the length, and so within the organization they are called 41's. They are designed to respond to any mission in seas of 8 feet or less and are the backbone of small boat stations across the country. Waves larger than 8 feet place the crew in extreme danger, and the boat becomes unstable. The counterbalanced, lead-bottomed, and therefore self-righting 47-footers are used in heavier seas.

"We're taking waves over the bow. My pumps can't keep up," Crawford told Station Gulfport.

"What's the weather like where you are?" the watch stander's voice came back, and Crawford described the conditions as another voice from over the radioman's shoulder instructed, "Hit the SAR alarm and launch the 41." This voice belonged to the officer of the day (OOD), the enlisted man in charge of the small boat station. He then calculated the distance from the small boat station to the *Bandit*, in this case about 25 miles, then factored in the weather and came to a troubling conclusion.

"I don't think the 41 will make it in time." He knew the 41 would take an hour to reach the boat at its top speed of 26 knots, but in the current conditions the coxswain (the enlisted person trained to operate the boat) would have to slow the boat to keep it afloat, stretching the time to several hours.

"Let me talk to the captain and get District on the horn. We're going to need a helicopter." The OOD keyed the microphone button and said, "Captain, we are getting our boat underway right now. Do you have life jackets on board?" The answer came back yes. "Do you have a life raft on board?"

"A hard foam ring with mesh net in the bottom," Crawford answered, knowing the Coast Guardsman was thinking that the *Bandit* would sink, and he and his crew would have to abandon ship. In other words they were in deep trouble.

"I'm going to ask you to do something unorthodox" the OOD said. "If you feel it is safe to do so, I want you to beach your boat on Ship Island." His wall-mounted chart showed this barrier island to the west of the cut they were trying to navigate.

"Uh, Coast Guard," Crawford said, "I think my wife Mattie is having a heart attack. Please hurry, she has a history of heart problems, and the stress is getting to her."

Meanwhile, the radioman was calling the SAR coordinator at the Rescue Center at District headquarters in New Orleans. The SAR coordinator, buried deep in a room full of charts, radios, and monitors on the Coast Guard grounds near downtown, has an up-to-the-minute report on the status of every Coast Guard boat and aircraft within the district, and it is his job to use those assets wisely. Each SAR case initiates a sequence of events and it is the coordinator's job to take whatever steps he deems proper. In this case one of his first steps was to request the launch ready helicopter.

That was us. The Air Station is in Belle Chasse, just south of the greater New Orleans area, about 20 miles from the SAR coordinator's office. Until he called our operations desk we were unaware of the events unfolding out at sea, but once that call came through an alert over the public address system sent us jumping.

"Put the ready helo on the line. Shrimper taking on water off Ship Island."

The watch captain bellowed instructions as we latched the small tow tractor to the tow bar on the nose of the aircraft. The line crewman held the button that opened the hangar door as the pilots charted the position of the *Bandit*. The flight mechanic and I raced with our gear toward the helicopter's open door. The pilots followed closely behind us. The aircraft commander, as the person in charge, bears the responsibility for every man in the crew and for those below. The co-pilot, still learning the tricks of the flying trade, is also the primary navigator and troubleshooter, which allows the aircraft commander to concentrate on flying. The flight mechanic is the single most important position in the aircraft, for he or she is the hoist operator. The rest of us could not complete our part of the mission without them.

The twin engine HH-65A is a French-built Aerospatiale helicopter originally designed as a corporate transport helicopter, and it was a modified version of this aircraft that we were about to pile into. It replaced the aging single-engine, Sikorsky H-52 Sea Guard, which had a top speed of 80 knots; the HH-65A can double that. The new aircraft was also very agile and was almost able to complete a barrel roll—it was fun to fly. But the HH-65 was not necessarily the best aircraft for the many other duties. The Coast Guard had bought 96 of them when catching drug runners was our priority, and its limitations would make our job a little more difficult that night. The working space inside the aircraft is only about 6 feet long and a little over 3 feet wide, leaving little room for survivors. Its small size did not require big, powerful engines to move it forward with great speed, but we needed that greater power to hoist multiple survivors. We could hoist two or three as long as the aircraft's tanks were not full of fuel, but we often had more survivors than we could hoist. The way I saw it, the Coast Guard had bought a sports car when what they really needed was a pickup.

The four of us jumped in, strapping the five-point harnesses around our bodies. Over the static of the internal communication system (ICS) I heard the pilot's metallic voices as they ticked off the items on the startup checklist. Soon the whine of the engine and thump of the blades became a steady beat. During startup I always tried to answer only direct questions so as to not create any distractions, taking this time to mentally complete my own checklist. "Did I forget my fins?" But once the blades started beating my heart started pumping.

In the air the aircraft commander briefed us on the mission at hand, as much as he knew. As happens on many SAR cases, especially in severe weather conditions, the difference between what is reported and what's actually happening maybe significant. We looked forward through the windshield as we sped towards the *Bandit* and could see the rain reflecting the flashing position lights of the aircraft—beyond that, nothing.

While we were bouncing through unstable air, buffeted by gusts and pelted by rain, the SAR coordinator completed another required step, an Urgent Marine Broadcast, which calls all ships in the area to help an endangered boat if they can. The captain of the gambling ship *Europa Jet* was just a few miles from the *Bandit* and made top speed toward the stricken fishing boat. Within minutes of answering the hail, Captain John M. Foretich, a mariner with 33 years of experience, was piloting his big ship as close as possible, but he could not follow the sinking boat into the shallows. Knowing that lives were in danger, he lowered a small boat with his ship's doctor on board, but the waves crashed over the exposed boat and slammed it into the side of the bigger ship. Fearing for the safety of his own crew, Captain Foretich gave up and ordered the boat back on board. Deciding the only other thing he could do was to block the relentless winds and sledge-hammering seas, he turned his ship sideways. The ship took heavy rolls while attempting to provide a lee, and in the darkened night he hoped to provide some relief, while the gamblers played on.

We arrived overhead of the *Bandit* within an hour of receiving the call from the District SAR coordinator. On scene we discovered the boat heeling to port about 45 degrees, waves breaking over the stern, the deck and pilothouse awash. It was resting on the sandy bottom, but the rear of the boat was still being lifted and dropped by the breaking seas. The bow of the ship had been pushed hard aground, almost on the beach, raising it higher than the stern. The waves were ramming the stern of the boat like a wrecking ball, green and white water exploding in spray toward the bow.

"I'm going to make a low, slow pass overhead, I want everybody to take a good look," Lt Tim Rourke ordered. He was the aircraft commander and sure of himself. "It looks like the only clear hoisting site is the bow."

The pounding waves obscured the aft portion of the *Bandit*, but with the bow slightly raised we agreed that the flight mechanic should lower me on the hoist cable down to the bow, where I was to release from the cable and prepare the survivors for rescue.

"I can hit that—no problem," the flight mechanic said. "We just need to be careful of the steel cable running from the mast to the bow."

Rourke said, "Good call, I didn't even see it until you pointed it out," then turned his attention to me and said, "Jerry, the boat is tilting to port pretty good, and I think we can keep you off the cable, but you'll have to fend for yourself if we get too close."

"No sweat. Let's do it. Do you want to hoist all four or what?"

"Let's get the heart-attack patient first and transport. We don't have the power or the room to get all four. And Jerry, I want you to go with the patient during transport. The rest of the crew will have to wait until we get back."

"Understood."

The plan sounded so simple until I leaned into the open helicopter door, hearing the moan of the wind and feeling the sharp stinging rain on my face. The *Bandit* was making sounds like breakfast cereal—snap, crackle, pop. I yanked the ICS cord from my helmet and waited for the hand signal from the flight mechanic. The rotor's high-pitched scream assaulted my ears—for me it's a comforting sound. The flight mechanic swept his arm toward the door, and I scuttled across the deck from my seat in the rear and sat in the open door, my feet dangling in the wind. I looked at the boat below where I was to package the patient for hoisting, mentally reviewing what I needed to do: treat life threats, major bleeding and trauma first, then place the patient in a litter or basket. Can she sit upright? Does she need oxygen? How much fuel do we have, and will I have time to finish this? My mind raced through the questions without waiting for answers. I would simply just have to react as the situation dictated.

The targeted landing area was a two-foot-square section of wood deck, somewhat protected from the breaking waves by the pilothouse. Slick with wind-swept rain, the deck was leaning, and the *Bandit* was far from still as it was twisted and slammed by the incoming seas. Rourke pointed the nose of the aircraft into the wind, using it to create lift and also placing the island behind and to the left of us. To an overhead observer, had there been one, the boat and helicopter would have looked like a T, the aircraft being the horizontal and the boat the vertical. From this position the boat was outside our right door.

The hoist cable stretched taut and I was lifted from the deck. I lowered my mask to protect my eyes from the rain and began swinging back and forth on the end of the hoist hook. *Bandit's* bow was bathed in the helicopter's floodlights. When I was about 8 feet from my ever-moving landing spot I had little choice but to snag the thick steel cable, the one the flight mechanic had noticed running from the bow to the main mast behind the pilothouse. Fortunately, though, I had learned to wear my wetsuit gloves during every rescue regardless of the temperature. Several months earlier I had grabbed another cable very similar to this one, only to find its strands burred out in all directions so that they ripped my bare palm into hamburger meat.

With the *Bandit* in my grip but before my feet were on solid deck the flight mechanic began rolling out hoist cable. I was on the wrong side of the boat from my intended landing mark and had to flip both legs over the steel cable. Once I gained footing on the lip of the anchor hold hatch I skidded to my knees with the grace of a wounded duck. When I finally stopped sliding I released the hoist hook and the flight mechanic retrieved it skyward. I stood and was just 10 feet in front of the pilothouse.

Everything was moving—the ship was swaying and the metal net booms rocked back and forth. I had to squint up into the blinding hover lights as I waited for the weight bag and trail line to be lowered to me. The trail line is a polypropylene line 105 feet long and on the delivery end a small brass snap hook with a weight bag holds 5 pounds of lead shot to keep it from blowing in the wind and rotor wash. Out of the darkness the bag swung into focus, fluttering in the beam of light, and now and then I could see the big white letters "USCG" on the bottom of the aircraft. The helicopter was preparing to deliver the basket with my emergency medical gear, so I gathered in the trail line hand over hand until I could retrieve the basket and unload my gear on deck.

The flight mechanic then hoisted the basket clear while I half-crawled, half-climbed down to the pilothouse and my patient. As I passed the windows of the pilothouse I noticed my reflection, mask still on my face, and realized that if I appeared out of the gloom like a big orange alien I could give the heart attack patient a fatal scare. I tilted the mask to my forehead.

With each step my wetsuit booties slipped on the tilted, moving deck as if it were covered in fish guts. A time or two I even looked down to make sure it was only wind, rain and waves as I slid down toward the port side of the pilothouse and the open cabin door, feet spread wide and hands gripping the rails. I spun around the open door to be greeted by the panic-stricken crewmen. Mattie sat on the deck next to the wheel, with Captain Crawford just inside the door, as the other two crewmen braced themselves in the shadows of the dimly lit cabin. Like most shrimpers working the Gulf, the pilothouse of the *Bandit* had a long narrow path from one door to the other, chart table behind the wheel and radios mounted overhead with flat vertical windows facing forward.

Captain Crawford said, "She was feeling weak and said it feels like another attack."

I knelt to talk to her. "What does the pain feel like? Is it only in your chest or elsewhere too?"

"My chest feels squeezed, and I can feel the pain all the way down to both hands," she said. "I also take nitro tabs for angina, but I didn't bring any for this trip."

"When was the last time you took the nitro?"

"I can't remember."

"How long have these symptoms been going on this time?"

"About an hour, but they're worse than usual."

Warning bells were ringing in my head. This might be a real heart attack and not just stress, but to make a definitive diagnosis was not my job. That would happen in a hospital, not on a shrimp boat being torn apart by the surf. It was up to me to make the best and quickest decision possible and provide the correct treatment that would keep Mattie alive long enough for a doctor to care for her.

"Captain," I said, "We need to get your wife out of here now," frantically considering the best way to transport my patient. I thought a semi-sitting position would be more comfortable for her than laying her flat and quickly discarded the idea of trying to hoist her in the litter. With the tilt of the boat, wind, and waves I didn't think we could pull that off.

"You're not going to leave us here are you?" one of Crawford's crewmen pleaded, his eyes bulging with fear.

"I have to. But I'll be back, you've got my word on it," I said. I could tell it was not a comfort. After Crawford shot the man a look that silenced him, the man turned away. One of the many lessons I had learned from other cases was that the tension in such an environment is often thick, like a crowd on the edge of a riot. My bullish confidence and actions might make the difference between success and mayhem.

I leaned down and checked Mattie's pulse as I spoke to her about what we needed to do. Her every action—how fast she was breathing, what she said—were signs, giving me clues to her true condition.

"Mattie, I'm going to put you in a basket. It will seem scary, but I need you to trust me. We know what we're doing, and this is like a ride at Disney World," I said though I doubted she had ridden any rollercoaster's for years.

"I'm going to have the helicopter hoist down a basket and bring it to the door. We'll place you in it and carry you out onto the deck. The worst part of this will be getting wet. I've found that if you're scared, it helps to just close your eyes. I'll be right beside you until the basket clears the deck." Reluctantly she agreed to let us hoist her off with a soft, "Okay." I stood and radioed the hovering helicopter 50 feet above my head, explaining what I wanted to do.

While I was on the *Bandit* the District SAR Coordinator was requesting a second helicopter from Belle Chasse, knowing our limited cabin space might prevent a timely rescue. Each air station is required to maintain one fully qualified crew 24 hours a day, and in most instances if a second crew is needed, they must be recalled from home. There is no guarantee that a full complement can be reached, despite the public's faith that when you call the Coast Guard, they will come. That night the officer manning the desk back at the air station was able to recall a pilot, co-pilot, and a flight mechanic, but unable to reach another rescue swimmer. The second aircrew launched and would arrive at the *Bandit* about 10 minutes after we were scheduled to return from our rendezvous with the ambulance. About the same time, the OOD at Station Gulfport had arranged for an ambulance to meet us at the local airport.

Many miles from all those players helping to ensure our success, I keyed the mike of my radio; "I'm ready for the basket." Our rescue basket is welded from polished stainless steel and floats with the aid of two round rolls of foam covered by red Cordura material.

I climbed out of the crowded pilothouse to find footholds wherever I could. With the *Bandit*'s nose shoved onto the sand and the stern being lifted and dropped by the breaking surf and the heavy leftward lean, I had to move downward to port then upward to starboard. The rain was still coming down in steady sheets, leaving the deck as slick as wet glass. With care gripped the handrail on the front of the pilothouse and pulled myself up to my earlier landing spot on the anchor-hold hatch, then slung one loose arm around the cable handrail that encompassed the ship and turned my eyes skyward. As the basket came screaming by my head, I snagged it and slammed it to the deck, leaving the cable attached, then carried it close to the door of the pilothouse.

"Mattie, get in," I yelled over the noise of the hovering helicopter. "You guys grab the other side. We can't hoist it from this spot, we need to be in the clear."

Crawford and the upset crewman grasped the sides of the basket. Mattie was a petite woman, and we were able to traverse the slippery deck quickly. The helicopter began creeping sideways; the open door where the flight mechanic knelt was getting closer. The screaming aircraft crept down closer to us to a hover 30 feet directly overhead, even before I gave the thumbs-up signal, to indicate Mattie and I were ready for the pickup. The cable went tight and then—despite the rain, wind, moving boat, and obstacles—Mattie was gingerly lifted from the deck. Once the basket was clear I signaled I was ready for pickup as well.

In a blur I was back in the helicopter and we were on our way to shore. I momentarily connected to the aircraft's ICS in order to pass Mattie's condition to the pilots. "We've got an ambulance waiting at an airport ten minutes from here, Jerry," Rourke replied. With the strong tailwinds, we landed in eight.

Once we were on deck we moved on fast forward, fearing there might be nothing left of the *Bandit*. Though not in direct communication with the small-boat crew during our brief stay on the tarmac we believed they were still making their way toward the *Bandit*. I was concentrating so hard on caring for Mattie I didn't remember the pilot telling me about the second aircraft, but by the time we were airborne again they were well on their way too.

Thirty minutes had passed while we delivered our patient, got fuel, and returned. The boat was still there, but we couldn't see any crewmen on deck. We hoped they had hunkered down in the pilothouse hiding from the storm and tried hailing them on the radio—no answer. What had gone wrong? Were they washed overboard, or did a brave civilian rescue them? We were anxious and quick to investigate.

When I hit the deck—hard—I noticed the difference immediately. The boat felt spongy, less sturdy, and sat much lower in the waves. From my landing spot on the deck I saw no survivors, and the ship had gone dark. I unclasped the hoist hook and held my open palm toward the sky, the signal for "I'm all right." I slid across the deck and caught the pilothouse door, thankful to see three wide-eyed faces expressing fear and wordless relief at seeing me again.

John Crawford said, "I didn't think you guys could make it back in time. The radio's dead, and she's coming apart." Constant pounding by the heavy breakers had finally broken the keel, and water had raced through the hull, filling the engine spaces, killing power and the radio.

My own radio crackled to life: Rourke asked, "Are they all right?"

"Roger that, three wet survivors ready for the basket. But we need to hurry, the boat is not doing well."

"The Coast Guard small boat had turned back, it's just us now," he said. I realized the heavy weather had made it too dangerous for them to continue. There would be no rescue boat as a backup.

Crouching in the pilothouse, I felt the boat rise from the rear as a steep, especially vicious wave pushed toward the beach. The bow of the *Bandit* punched the sand with a thud, a shuddering vibration shot through the deck, and we heard wood cracking, splintering. The boat quivered for a second as the wave passed the bow, then settled back onto the bottom.

"Time to go," I said into the radio. With my mind still calculating all the angles of this rescue, I worried about the helicopter's ability to hoist all four of us. I knew we had neither the power nor the room. Had I known about the launch of second aircraft, I would have worried less about the possibility that my survivors and I might be going for a swim. Rourke and the rest of my crew, meanwhile, thought I knew about the second aircraft.

I shouted instructions to each crewman and told them to come out onto the deck one at a time when I waved my hand. Then I clambered back to the hoisting site and again wrapped my right arm around the steel handrail cable. My right shoulder was almost touching the deck. If the boat had been level I would have been lying down. Though it would have been much easier to control the basket with both hands, there was no way I could let go of that cable. I surely would have been tossed overboard by the waves, because they were, by that point, crashing over the length of the boat.

When I waved to the man watching from the pilothouse window, he nearly sprinted across the deck and jumped into the basket. I held it until it cleared the bow cable and was on its way up. In seconds the empty basket came back, and the second hoist went just as smoothly. Captain Crawford's crewmen were safe, but I watched with mounting anxiety as my helicopter, my lifeline and ride home, slowly hover-taxied forward and disappeared into sheets of rain.

Before I could grab my radio and—politely—ask for a new course of action, the second aircraft crept out of the dark skies like an angel shrouded in light, illuminated by its floodlights. I gave the ready signal immediately, for I was indeed ready. I should have been cold, but I was sweating as Crawford and I anxiously waited our turns. With each passing minute the deck became softer; boards were shifting and cracking under my weight. The lights of the hovering helicopter lit up debris that moments earlier had been the bottom of the boat, now scattered outward in the breaking waves. I thought we might end up going for a swim at any second. If the *Bandit* failed to hold together for a few more minutes that swim would be our last, the waves too powerful for our feeble human bodies.

The last planks of the deck were coming apart as I watched Captain Crawford disappear above my head. The flight mechanic hurriedly dropped the basket with Crawford still inside onto the helicopter deck, then sent the bare hook right back down even sooner than I expected.

A bare-hook recovery is considered an emergency; no communication is necessary between helicopter crew and swimmer. If a hook is lowered, the swimmer gets on it no matter what. I grabbed the hook without waiting for it to hit the deck. As a rule we tried to let the hoist hook contact the water or some other grounding point, such as a boat, to discharge its built-up static electricity, but this time I didn't wait. Even though my neoprene gloves blocked the full charge, I felt as if I had stuck my finger into a light socket.

I yanked the D ring from its slot in the harness wrapped around my chest and snapped it on the hook. Looking upward, I gave my trademark two thumbs up, but before the flight mechanic could lift me, the rear of the boat rose like a shark lunging for its meal—and I was that meal. The deck buckled but held long enough for the slack in the hoist cable to be taken up. I was hoisted clear with the boat still coming at me; a wave was shoving it toward the beach as the pilot simultaneously backed the aircraft in the same direction. To compound the problem, the boat climbed skyward, canceling my sensation of moving up. Even though the flight mechanic was reeling in hoist cable like an excited fisherman with the catch of a lifetime, I couldn't clear the deck by more than two feet.

It was as if the *Bandit*, cheated of her victims, was determined to take me in their place. The aircrew could see what was happening and attempted to gain clearance for me by moving shoreward, toward the bow. I began sailing with great speed through the air and, from the corner of my eyes, glimpsed the forward stanchion on the bow.

Its steel arms welded to a heavy post jutted up and out from the deck and stood in my path. Reacting automatically, grunting and heaving, I brought my knees and legs into the tightest sit-up of my life, almost touching my face. Still I could see I wasn't going to make it. Hanging from the hoist hook with my knees touching my chin my backside was the lowest part of my body, and in a split second was about to slam into the post. At 60 knots of air speed I was about to create an explosion of blood and tissue. I closed my eyes as I braced for the impact; instead I felt only rushing air. I gave a twisting backward glance in time to see the boat disappear into the blackness.

The captain of the *Europa Jet* said, "It broke into a million pieces." He later reported finding debris scattered for miles.

I was greeted at the door of the helicopter by the toothy grin of one of the best flight mechanics in the Coast Guard, John "Flash" Gordon. When I began the wild ride off the boat I had no idea who was working the hoist on the second helicopter, but I was immensely glad to see his friendly face. He saved my butt, literally.

About a week later I called the hospital where Mattie had been taken, trying to learn of her condition. Like all non-relatives, I was given just the information that was considered public. She had been admitted and was receiving treatment. At least I had the satisfaction of knowing she survived.

CHAPTER 2

Life and Death

When I was a teenager I gave Death a face. I conjured a mental picture, drawing from the most widely known archetypes, and gave him the ability to take whatever form he desired. Sometimes he was a car wreck, or a thief, or the cold dark raging sea. Always, though, he was, in my mind, the embodiment of darkness versus light, evil versus good, wrong versus right. But to acknowledge the blackness that is death, I was forced to accept the opposite view; life is the scorching white light that is good. That good—that rightness—had soldiers. Paramedics, firemen, doctors, and countless others were all fighting to preserve life.

This awakening did not occur at the passing of my great-grandmother, Della Roberts, when I was seven. I was told she went to live in Heaven, how could that be bad? Later, in the eighth grade, a friend's older brother died in his sleep (so I was told). Yet this seemed surreal and did not cause me great anguish. I was not awakened to the emotional turmoil concerning the reality of death until 1983, at the age of seventeen. This great emotional response, despite all the horrors of the world that could have sparked it in me, was caused by the widely broadcast news story of the sinking of the *Marine Electric*. That was the moment my psyche was scarred.

Sitting at my home in Plant City, Florida I watched and read the news stories with great interest, especially the Coast Guard's part in it, envisioning, feeling the anguish and terror of drowning in the belly of that ship, or freezing to death, or being devoured by sharks. I was unaware of the profound affect this event would have on my life both emotionally, and in the long term, physically. The sinking of the

Marine Electric, a turning point for the Coast Guard, was in fact my true beginning.

On Thursday, 10 February 1983, the *Marine Electric* was moored in the Elizabeth River and surrounded by the sprawling naval complexes of Norfolk, Virginia. Her 605-foot hull was tied to the Norfolk and Western Railroad terminal pier with 24,800 tons of coal evenly distributed throughout its holds. The ship was to deliver her cargo to the electrical power plant in Brayton Point, Massachusetts.

Wind and rain greeted the crew as they set course for the open sea. Gale warnings had been posted from Cape Henlopen to Virginia Beach, calling for Force 8 winds (34-40 knots) from the northeast. Worse yet, the weather was expected to deteriorate to a Force 10 (minimum winds of 50 knots).

At 38 years old, the *Marine Electric* was one of the oldest ships of her kind still plying the coastal routes of the United States.

Every ship has particular things that must be secured or set when it puts to sea. The closing of hatches, settings of the engines, even the making of coffee are just a few elements known as setting the sea detail. As part of the sea detail the crew of the *Marine Electric* was required to secure the accordion folding hatches used to protect the cargo. These hatches had become much harder to lock down after replacement of the worn hatch cover gaskets with ill-fitting new ones during the ship's last dry dock in 1981. They were enormous, almost as wide as the ship and vital to the watertight integrity of the boat's cargo areas.

As the ship crossed over the Chesapeake Bay Bridge Tunnel the wind was worse than had been forecasted. The *Marine Electric* plowed through 25-foot seas and blizzard conditions all night and late into the next day, riding well and shedding water from her decks as designed.

On Friday afternoon at 3:30 PM she passed to the west of the 65-foot fishing boat *Theodora*. The freighter was following the usual shipping lanes 30 miles offshore, running north and parallel to the coast, while the *Theodora* was struggling westward attempting to reach safety and escape the storm. Shortly after the ships passed, the *Theodora*—having taken as much abuse as it could handle—began to fill with seawater. The crew of the stricken fishing boat radioed the Coast Guard requesting immediate assistance, and as was (and still is) its practice, the Coast Guard hailed other ships in the area to render help, according to the time honored tradition, even in times of war, of mariners lending a hand to fellow seafarers. Captain Corl, acting master of the *Marine Electric*, responded to the hail when the Coast Guard watch stander asked, "Captain can you divert from your present course to assist?" Corl agreed.

At 4:10 PM on 11 February he commanded the ship to change course and shadow the *Theodora*, so that if the crew of the fishing boat had to abandon ship they could pick them up right away. He warned the Coast Guard the *Marine Electric* might roll in the existing seas, but ordered the course change anyway, and stayed with the *Theodora* until 7:00 PM the same evening, when the Coast Guard was able to hoist a pump to the fishing boat.

With the *Marine Electric* released from her escort duties, Corl ordered the ship to set a northeasterly course of 040 degrees. The seas had built to 25 feet and were breaking onto the #2 hatch, coaming and rolling all the way to the #4 hatch. The waves were breaking on the bow, and the ship was plowing through them rather than riding up. When the watch stander noticed the bow was not rising as high as it had been, he roused Corl from a nap on a settee on the back of the bridge.

After observing the ship's ride Corl went below and woke the chief mate, who hustled to the deck, took one look, and ran down to wake the chief engineer.

All were troubled by the way the ship was settling at the bow, together they tried to discover the reason for the worsening ride.

"Go wake all the men, have them dress in heavy clothes and muster on deck," the chief mate ordered one of the able-bodied seamen.

Still unable to determine a cause, they recognized the clear danger. Corl ordered a course change to 000 degrees due north, then called the Coast Guard at 2:51 AM.

"Coast Guard, this is the *Marine Electric*. We are experiencing some settling by the bow and request a helicopter be sent to illuminate the ship. It will help us determine the gravity of the situation."

"Ready the lifeboats," Corl ordered the chief engineer as a precaution.

Again Corl reported to the Coast Guard, "I think the forward hatch has broken in and my forward decks are awash. I got uncontrolled flooding from unknown sources."

Twenty-five minutes later the ship begun to list to starboard about five degrees, then ten degrees by 4:11 AM. The outcome was inevitable. Corl knew it, and at 4:13 AM he ordered the crew to abandon ship, radioing the Coast Guard as the crew donned lifejackets.

"We are abandoning ship right now! We are abandoning ship right now!" came the last transmission from the *Marine Electric*.

The *Marine Electric* did not give her crew the chance to safely abandon ship. She rolled abruptly onto her side, immersing thirty-four men a killing field of icy water.

The radio watch standers at Coast Guard Group Eastern Shore and Small Boat Station Ocean City, Maryland, had been in continuous communication with the freighter until all radio communications ceased at exactly 4:13 AM 12 February 1983. Throughout the escalation of events they had been feverishly contacting numerous rescue resources. The cutter *Point Highland*, an 82-foot patrol boat, was dispatched from Chincoteague, Virginia.

To broaden the rescue attempt the Group passed coordination of the effort to the Coast Guard District Five Operations Center in Portsmouth, Virginia. From this centralized location the Coast Guard had a greater number of assets at its disposal. The 205-foot seagoing tug cutter *Cherokee* was released from a law-enforcement patrol in waters off New York and began steaming southward.

Another 82-foot boat, the cutter *Point Arena*, was made underway from Station Little Creek, Virginia. An HH-3 helicopter, commonly referred to as the Pelican, was launched from Elizabeth City, North Carolina; this was the same helicopter that had earlier dropped a pump to the *Theodora*.

The Coast Guard personnel coordinating the rescue did not stop there. Via an Urgent Marine Broadcast they requested two other ships to divert from their position to render assistance. (An Urgent Marine Broadcast is used by the Coast Guard to relay information of a life or death nature to ships at sea.) The merchant ship *Tropic Sun* and freighter *Berganger* also responded and set courses for the *Marine Electric*.

The Navy diverted the USS *Jack Williams*, an Oliver Perry Class Guided Missile Cruiser, and the USS *Seattle*, a Tennessee Class

Armored Cruiser; both ships were operating 70 miles east of the shipping lanes.

The Coast Guard was bearing down on the crippled freighter with every asset the U.S. Government could muster, with one notable exception: Coast Guard rescue swimmers did not yet exist.

When the Coast Guard HH-3 helicopter was first to arrive, at 5:20 AM, the District Operations Center personnel learned that the crew of the *Marine Electric* had not made it to the lifeboats. Strobe lights blinked from the water, flashing their deadly message to the rescuers above. Some of the lights were attached to empty life rafts, others to motionless crewmen. Repeatedly and with great difficulty, the helicopter crew lowered the rescue basket to the apparently lifeless forms. Reportedly, some of the men in the water were in the final stages of hypothermia and lacked the strength to climb into the basket. The aircrew—a pilot, co-pilot, flight mechanic (hoist operator), and an avionicsman (communications and navigation)—had no means to deploy a rescuer into those conditions. Of the 34 souls, they were able to pick up just one, the third mate, from a life raft.

At the request of the helicopter crew and Coast Guard District, a Navy H-3 helicopter was launched from Naval Station Little Creek, Virginia, with a Navy rescue swimmer, James D. MacCann, on board. They arrived on scene at 6:15 AM.

MacCann entered an oil-slicked, storm-tossed ocean, efficiently killing all in its grasp. He saved two men barely clinging to life, then recovered numerous bodies of the less fortunate. The would-be rescue ships converged on the scene at first light, only to become the transport for the body bags.

The third mate later reported, "I was thrown into the water, I looked up and saw Captain Corl climbing over the rail as the ship was rolling…This was the last time I saw the Captain."

Corl's body was never found. He and six others were lost at sea that morning, while 24 dead men and two more survivors were plucked from the water.

The hull of the *Marine Electric* remained visible until approximately 11:00 AM, when it sank in 120 feet of water in position 37-53.1 North; 74-46.4 West.

The story of the *Marine Electric* has been repeated, in hushed tones, throughout the Coast Guard since that fateful night, retold definitively by award-winning writer Robert Frump in his book *Until the Sea Shall Free Them.*

In 1983, because of the lessons learned, Congress mandated the Coast Guard to implement a program enabling helicopter crews to deploy a physically capable person into any conditions and rescue those in distress. Thus began the Coast Guard Rescue Swimmer Program.

The *Marine Electric* saga captivated me, and I devoured every scrap of news I could find about it, yet for three years after the tragedy of the *Marine Electric* that was all the action I took. Since my awakening to Death's reality I attempted to find satisfaction in earning money at a furniture store and obtaining my degree, failing at both— my grades were abysmal and my boss was the one making the money. My hair was long, my face ten years too young to be taken seriously. But I continued to show up for work, loyal as a dog, all the while thinking "Is this all there is? Work to make money and study so I can be better at making money?"

Doubts nibbled at my mind while I pondered my future, until a brush with Death itself woke me up.

A fellow a couple of years older than me had bought a very expensive TV on credit from the store, and when he fell behind on his payments I was sent to repossess it. Repossessing furniture requires more art than muscle, as the item or items are usually inside someone's home. For that reason the store had a policy of wiping the slate clean upon the return of the financed item, regardless of condition. I found it helpful to be able to tell the delinquent he would not be reported to the credit bureau, and that he might even obtain financing from the same store again. This time, after I explained this policy to my customer, he told me to go to his house and pick up the set, saying that when he got back on his feet he would catch up on the payments and take the same TV back. I was glad he saw reason, as it made my unpleasant task more palatable.

I drove to his house, parked, and walked up to the front door. After my knock, a man I did not recognize answered the door saying he knew nothing about a TV.

"You must have the wrong address," he said.

Back to my Jeep I went to double-check. It was the correct address, so I drove to a nearby convenience store and called our customer at his work.

"I'm only a couple of miles from the house," he said. "I'll be right there."

I timed my return to coincide with his and had just come to a stop when his car, a mid 1970's Oldsmobile, came careening around the corner. Dirt and grass went flying as he slid across the yard. He jumped out yelling. Unable to hear what he was saying, I stepped out anyway, hoping to get the TV and be on my way.

The same hostile young man yanked open the door, yelling, "You don't have no TV here." My customer was all worked up, his emotions high, tears streaming down his face.

"You guys can kick me out, but that TV is mine, you bastards."

The biggest man inside the house took a step toward him from the open door. I lost count of how many faces I saw inside and had no idea why they all suddenly backed up. Then I saw it; my customer had pulled a small handgun out of his pocket and was moving toward the door.

"Oh shit, oh shit," I thought, backing toward my Jeep.

My customer turned and pointed the gun at my retreating body. "Where the hell you going? Get this damn TV," he sobbed. He stepped inside, and I could still hear him screaming, though I couldn't make out what he was saying. He grabbed the edge of the TV with his free hand and began rolling it end over end out of the front room and down the sidewalk. I quickly realized it would be easier and safer to help than to run and moved forward to help him. He and I loaded the TV, and I jumped in the front seat and roared out of the neighborhood without looking back.

I was shaking, so I had to pull to the side of the road, where I sat for two hours just thinking, "This wasn't like the movies. Should I have run? I can't hide from death. I could die at any moment, so how do I make what time I have count?" These and a thousand other thoughts filled my head.

The sidelines of life were safe, and if I hung in there eventually I would make lots of money. But was that how I wanted to live, relying on others to keep me safe, to fight my fight? Could I do something that made a difference? On the side of that road I naïvely decided that, with the proper training and dedication, I could defeat death. In my mind, that was exactly what all those in the emergency response field did. Still deep in thought, I remembered the news stories of the *Marine Electric* and how the Coasties seemed to jump into the middle of the most challenging conditions imaginable. They were on the front lines, and I wanted to join them.

But I still had doubts. Was I able to join an organization like the Coast Guard and make a difference, or would I become just another cog in their machine? Was I deluding myself? Mostly, I wondered whether I was worthy.

Then just a couple of months before my enlistment date, I watched in horror with the rest of the world as the space shuttle *Challenger* blew up. Death had morphed into yet another tragic new form, and the Coast Guard in the news again. They were searching, albeit without success, for the lost astronauts. On that cold February morning I knew that I had made the right decision. A few weeks later, in April of 1986, I left for Coast Guard boot camp.

CHAPTER 3

The Test

The next summer, 1987, I drove into the small Southern coastal town of Elizabeth City, North Carolina, admiring the picturesque trees and vintage country homes nestled along the Pasquotank River. The town's roots were tied to the surrounding farms and the area's largest employer, the U.S. Coast Guard.

The Coast Guard base, south of town, comprises the main aircraft parts warehouse, small boat station, support command, air station, and training center. It was at the Aviation Technical Training Center (ATTC), where enlisted Coasties go to learn their aviation jobs, that I was transformed into a Coast Guard rescue swimmer.

That first night and for a month afterwards my classmates and I were thrust together in a large barracks bunkroom known as a squad bay. It was spacious enough to provide eighteen of us with a rack, locker, and desk apiece. Eventually we would be reassigned to three-person rooms, almost suites by comparison. The barracks, known as the Doughnut, was a circular, three-story block building, wrapped around a plot of grass, which when full probably held two hundred Coasties.

The school on the opposite side of the base was a nondescript, fairly new building resembling a small community college. Its halls were polished to a high gloss in strict military fashion; everything was very orderly. Outside its walls we received the first of a never-ending number of physical training (PT) tests.

The test began innocently. We were required to complete as many pushups, sit-ups, and pull-ups as possible with each portion limited to two minutes. We also had to run 1½ miles in less than 14 minutes and swim 500 yards in less than 12 minutes. The instructors required us to complete the test without a break, to give them a baseline of each person's abilities. At that time there were no minimums to stay in the training.

The Coast Guard instructors provided us with the basics of our new job: parachute packing, liferaft repair, and basic lifesupport equipment maintenance, but relied on the Navy to train us as helicopter rescue swimmers. Navy swimmer training was conducted at the Naval Air Station in Pensacola, Florida. My Coast Guard instructors had recently established fitness minimums we had to meet before we could go on to the Navy Rescue Swimmer School.

In 1987, the program was so new that most of our Coast Guard instructors had not yet gone to the swimmer school themselves. Our guides were flying blind and navigating by feel. But they knew the rigors of the school we faced and tailored our training sessions to meet the minimums of the Navy school's physical fitness Out Test. This test included 50 shoulder-width pushups, 60 sit-ups, 5 pull-ups, 5 chin-ups, 1½ miles run in less than 12 minutes, a 500-yard swim in less than 12 minutes, four 25-yard underwater laps, ½ mile buddy-tow swim, and a 1-mile flight-suit swim.

They focused on meeting those standards and to graduate as many as possible in order to accomplish the Coast Guard's goal of bringing rescue swimmers to Coast Guard Aviation by the end of 1988. However, the instructors steadfastly refused to lower those standards to fill billets. They never allowed someone who was unable to do the job to make it through the school. Those who quit during this build-up phase were allowed to return to fleet as unrated workers and request new job training. This request was known as D.O.R., Drop On Request. A few candidates were also removed involuntarily because they were unable to meet the minimums. This mindset, and the training that accompanied it, whittled our number from eighteen down to twelve.

Once we were ready and the appointed time had arrived, because the Navy could not accommodate all twelve at once, we were split into two groups of six and shipped off to Pensacola two weeks apart. I left with the first six the second week of November 1987.

The front gate of the Naval Station in Pensacola sent shivers of nervous anticipation down our spines. We stopped and took a picture by the sign, fearing not all of us would make it through the training. We wanted proof we had made it at least as far as Pensacola.

I stood next to friends like Dan "Pappy" Lanihan, called Pappy because he was the oldest at twenty-nine. I laugh now, to have thought of him as old. Irish through and through, he shamed us with his ability to drink till sun-up, then outrun or outswim everyone. Hub Ross sported spiked hair while off duty and was always smiling. I owe him a debt I'll never forget. Rob Rea, my roommate from Elizabeth City, was short and tough. After finishing his tour of duty with the Coast Guard he would join the Army and learn to fly attack helicopters. As for Kevin Peterson, you could almost hear the ladies' pounding hearts when Kevin entered a room. Happily married, he just ignored the sighs of the lovesick. A guy named Hudson, the strong silent type who kept to himself, did his time and moved on. A 130-pound stick of a boy, I felt out of place among these men, but I could swim.

The Navy's swimmer school was housed in an old red brick building with an indoor pool, five lanes wide and 12 feet deep. The deck of the pool was cluttered with flight helmets, harnesses, parachutes, and a training tower resembling a helicopter that pumped water downward to simulate rotor wash. A chain hanging over the deep end was used to dunk a mock aircraft into the water. This training tank was dark and sinister-feeling, and it made the hair on my neck stand on end. The smell of chlorine and sweat hung in the air. The deck around the pool was anything but a recreational place. We had not come here for fun.

The first day of class 33 students lined up on the sidewalk outside the double wood doors, most of them young recruits fresh from the Navy's Aircrew School. Two more Coasties, "rolled" from a previous class also joined us. (To be rolled meant the instructors felt you were not progressing and decided to restart you with the next convening class.)

We had noticed a small trench in the grass about four feet in front of us, 6 inches wide and two or three inches deep. With murmured speculation we were guessing as to what had caused such an unusual indentation when a grizzly of a man in gray sweats and a well-worn ball cap bearing the name of his last ship stormed from the building and called us to attention. We would later come to know him as the Anti-Christ, a nickname given him earlier by students. He moved his

250 pounds mounted on a 6' 4" frame as if awakened too early from a winter nap. He was looking for a head to bite off. The first Navy man he came to was shaking at his approach. The young Navy recruit stood at attention, arms to his sides, eyes staring into nothingness, sweating in the cool morning air.

"You look like shit, sailor, hit the deck!" he roared in a voice that reverberated through our bones. From the corners of our eyes we watched the recruit jump to the ground and assume the pushup position. When he landed, his hands rested in that shallow trench.

From the steps of the school boomed another voice, "What the hell are the rest of you pukes looking at? One of your teammates is on the ground. Join him! Now!"

It was another instructor who I'm convinced was deformed, his forearms thick as tree trunks. We later learned he had failed out of BUDs, the first phase of selection for SEAL training (Basic Underwater Demolition training) and took it personally. So began our four weeks of hell on earth.

For four days we learned escapes and releases, essential methods of breaking the hold of a panic-stricken survivor. When true fear takes hold, be it real or imagined, the human body reacts by releasing adrenaline. People in extreme fear can have superhuman strength and often attempt to use you, the rescuer, as an island by tightly clinging to your head. The instructors were trying to re-create this intensity in a game they had dubbed "Sharks and Daisies." We were not the sharks.

We were ordered to swim circles in the deep end of the pool with eyes closed and hands behind our backs, and complete an escape or release, whichever the instructor would yell in our ear, as he grabbed hold. This was the game, but the instructors followed no rules.

It was during that game we were introduced to Jason of *Friday the Thirteenth* horror-flick fame. One of the instructors wore a similar hockey mask and stayed hidden under the artificial helicopter spray created by the tower until a student had just completed a maneuver and looked winded. Then he would propel himself off the side of the pool and land on the student's head, wrapping his arm around his victim's neck.

Later that day the game had dwindled our number down to 20 students. With each new session of the game four or five instructors entered the pool. Often they grabbed individuals milliseconds apart, squeezing the student's neck like an anaconda. The instructors sensed our fear the way a lion feels its prey's panic just before the deathblow. When the instructors became bored of toying with us, they left the pool and relaxed while making us swim underwater laps. Tired and scared, some of us could not swim the length of the pool underwater, so rather then eliminate those unable to swim the length of the pool, the instructors made us lock arms and swim as one, telling us this underwater drill would continue until we had all completed four consecutive laps. We were also told to lock down on the arms of any man who tried to surface for air. Only then could we end this drill.

After each new drill it seemed someone was creeping toward The Bell. The Bell, forged from polished brass, was rung every time a person quit. When it happened the entire class dropped what they were doing and lined up in the building foyer to watch the quitter ring The Bell. He had to rap it three times and say, "I quit," after each metallic tone. Many often did so with tears running down their cheeks. We hung our heads, not in shame, but in fear that any one of us might be next. I feared I might be next. After the last tone, we were ordered to turn our back on the quitter as he left the building for the last time. The effect was emotionally draining. Fight or flight—each man had to choose.

Escapes and releases had a dark side that came to light during regular training and during the game of Sharks and Daisies. It happened so often that we gave it a nickname. Smurfing, we called it, after the cartoon of the same name. When one of the students did not do the move correctly while underwater, the instructor simply refused to let go. Either the student would think through the mistake and re-do it, or the instructor would haul him to the surface for negative reinforcement (pushups) or the student would pass out underwater. If it was the latter, then the student often turned blue—smurfing.

During one of the last games of Sharks and Daisies, after many stops to hear The Bell ring, I heard Kevin Peterson groan almost inaudibly, "My side is cramping." But Jason, hiding in the spray of the tower with hockey mask in place, heard and yelled, "Menstrual cramps!" while pointing at Kevin.

Weakness in any form was reason enough for the instructors to pounce. Each instructor dropped the student in his grasp and turned on Kevin like sharks in frenzy. The Anti-Christ's heavy footfalls as he ran from the pool office thundered over the screams of the Navy candidate next to Kevin. This young Navy man thought he was about to be caught up in the melee surrounding the Coastie. Kevin was helplessly wrapped from head to toe by instructors when the Anti-Christ jumped through the air, grabbed the chain hanging from the ceiling, and swung Tarzan style to land on the pile. They sank as one big entangled group to the bottom of the 12-foot pool. It was impossible for Kevin to complete an escape or release with so many arms wrapped around him. My mind was raced. I thought they had killed him.

The next instant the air was filled with the sound of thrashing water, and I opened my eyes to see what had happened. The instructors had an unwritten rule: no one was allowed to open his eyes. Opening your eyes invited unwanted attention. I saw four instructors on their knees pulling Kevin's limp, blue body from the water. The Anti-Christ stood over them, watching. Another instructor was in the water pushing Kevin up. The instructor kneeling over Kevin opened his airway, tilted his head back, and was about to start mouth-to-mouth resuscitation when the gurgling sound that precedes vomiting stopped him. Kevin gagged, coughed, and spewed bile-tinted pool water. Under his own power he rolled to his hands and knees. His body had automatically started breathing once the air passage was opened.

"Get back in the pool or quit," the Anti-Christ told him. Kevin's head hung loosely on his shoulders; down on all fours, he simply rolled back into the water without comment.

That was the moment I became convinced I was going to die. Every day for the next three weeks I woke up and said, "Today is a good day to die, let's get started!"

I thought the training could not get any harder. I was wrong.

The first four days lasted about ten hours each. None of us could keep food down, so we routinely skipped breakfast and lunch, opting instead to load up on multivitamins during the day and as many calories as possible after class ended. Friday morning, the fifth day of school, was Hell Day. We were, in traditional military fashion, roused from our slumber well before the first hints of sunlight on the horizon. The instructors were screaming and jumping excitedly about, motivating us to move faster and faster still.

We were herded to the sidewalk in front of the school where we went through every physical exercise known to man. After several hours, about breakfast time, the deformed torturer with the tree-trunk forearms lost interest. He stopped the training and instructed us to pick up a red brick in each hand from a small stack next to the building. We were required to hold them at arm's length while the instructors went inside to eat. Drop a brick, even a couple of inches, and they fanatically yelled at you from the Sharks Den, the office overlooking the sidewalk.

Despite not being able to feel my arms, I prayed breakfast would last for a couple of hours. I dreaded whatever they would come up with next.

An instructor renowned for his unbelievable ability to run in combat boots skidded to a halt in front of the school behind the wheel of a small pickup truck. Evidently this was what we were waiting for.

The bricks were left behind as the Boot Runner instructed us to keep up. He sprinted from the school, and in no time there were stragglers as we spread out. This did not escape the notice of the other instructor following us in a little white government truck. Their punishment was swift and varied—pushups until our faces fell to the dirt or flutter kicks until we were unable to stand upright. To complete flutter kicks we lay on our backs, hands under our buttocks, and held our feet 6 inches off the deck. Once the instructor started the exercise we pointed our toes, locked our knees, and kicked our legs up and down, never touching the ground. If one of us touched the ground we had to start over. They said this exercise worked our hip flexor muscles and helped the body make most efficient use of the swim fins. All I remember was how bad it hurt.

We were a motley bunch, covered in sand and with grass stuck to our sweaty bodies when we showed up for the Navy's mandatory flu shots. Annually the Navy requires that all personnel must receive flu shots. In order to accommodate many members at once, the medical department had set up numerous tables in the middle of a baseball field, each manned by corpsmen with needles. We stayed in the pushup position until it was our turn, when smirking corpsmen stuck us, with great pleasure, in our right arms. The others in the field looked upon us as lepers, shock and disbelief registering on their faces as they gave us a wide berth. No one seemed to care that we Coasties had already received flu shots, and we didn't press the point.

Rest eluded us, but not the instructors. About every other mile, the instructor leading the run jumped in the truck and a fresh one got out. They knew it was impossible to keep up, and that was the point.

About mid-morning, as the disciplinary exercises became repetitive, the Anti-Christ whipped the truck to a halt in front of the running formation next to a construction site. Gleefully, he picked up a chunk of former sidewalk. He halted us and ceremoniously presented Airman Rock. The 50-pound piece of cement he had dubbed Airman Rock was to accompany us everywhere.

As we ran it became brutally apparent no one could carry Airman Rock for more than about thirty seconds. All attempts to do so caused the man carrying it to lag behind, an unacceptable action for our collective well-being, as the instructors doled out negative reinforcement to the group, not individually. We shared the burden by passing the rock around.

We carried the boulder up overpass embankments, into crashing surf, through every obstacle in the course. By the end of the eighth hour my feet were shuffling along the ground and I began to lag behind. I was never known for my running prowess and the morning had taken its toll. About to fall down, I grabbed Hub Ross's grass-stained shirttail. I was dizzy. Hub intentionally hid my slumped-over body from the lead instructor and the others in the truck with his large frame. I would not have survived till lunch had it not been for Hub. As I said, I owe him.

The noon break was my turning point. The 20-minute reprieve and knowledge that we would spend the afternoon in the pool gave me the chance to rest and build my resolve. Putting me in the pool was like throwing Br'er Rabbit in the briar patch. I was going to make it through Hell Day.

The pool had its own stories to tell. It started when our new classmate Airman Rock sailed through the air and landed in the deep end, causing an upward explosion of water. Everything had to be rescued from the bottom, be it the rock or the old-fashioned school desk thrown in later.

The school desk was made of metal and wood and had a cubbyhole for books. We were required to lift the desk over our heads and swim upward until all four legs broke the surface. It was the instrument of demise for a couple of sailors unable to complete the task. They too rang The Bell.

I was at home in the water and felt that if I was going to survive, this was my greatest chance. The instructors seemed to have an endless supply of new and exciting ways to test both our endurance and desire to continue.

We knew, while still in Elizabeth City, that we would be required to complete certain swims and had practiced towing another person for half a mile and swimming 2000-yards while wearing a flight suit and boots. We didn't realize the Navy instructors would require those same swims and several others once we were near death.

As darkness fell the survivors of Hell Day were formed up in the pool, nut to butt. Each class member treaded water in the deep end while another treaded water directly behind him. In unison we counted off "One" and swam to the side of the pool as a unit. "Two," we lifted ourselves up onto the poolside, arms fully extended. "Three," we spun around and sat on the side, lifting our legs free of the water. When we finally did this perfectly, one of the instructors ordered the class leader to take charge of his class and dismiss them for the day. The class leader was the senior man in the class. The position was in constant state of flux, as the senior man was replaced when he screwed up or quit. Our class leader changed so often I cannot recall who this was.

I looked at the survivors and counted twelve. It was then I had an awakening. The measuring scale used by the Navy was not the same gauge used by the Coast Guard. The Navy instructors had lost their way. The Coast Guard would have seen the number of people falling by the way as wasteful, yet that seemed to be the point of this school. The more men they could make quit, the more successful they believed they were.

After coming to this conclusion, I decided not to contribute to their notion of success. The only way they could prevent me from graduating was to carry me out in a body bag. I now believe that forging the mentality of refusing to fail, no matter the consequences, was one of many secondary goals of the Navy swimmer program.

Late in my third week I saw Will Crown, another roommate from

Elizabeth City, sitting in the same little white truck from our Hell Day. Will was the youngest member of our original Coast Guard class of 12 and known for his easy-going smile. He and the rest of my class had arrived as scheduled, two weeks behind us. While in Elizabeth City he learned that one of his wrists had a hairline crack, making pushups extremely painful. The Coast Guard instructors almost removed him from school, but allowed him to stay if he did all his pushups on his knuckles. This was Will's idea, as the thought of giving up was more unpalatable. By the time he reached Pensacola he was able to do 120 knuckle pushups within two minutes. I think he could have done more if given more time. Will was tough.

As Will sat in the truck looking through the air not acknowledging anyone, it seemed as if he was semi-conscious. When we visited Will in the hospital later, he said the doctor told him he would have been dead from heat stroke in a matter of minutes had he not been brought in when he was. He also told us the Navy instructors had singled him out because of his style of pushups and decided to make him quit.

Our home for sit-ups was the ancient seawall behind the school. Jagged from years of exposure it gouged our bodies, exacting its due in blood from our backs and buttocks. Early in Week Three, while doing sit-ups, one of our instructors noticed a jellyfish infestation in the bay so thick that one could almost walk across the water on their backs. After a moment of collaboration, the instructors ran us down the seawall for about a mile and ordered us to enter the water and swim back. When we came out of the sea our eyes were almost swollen shut, welts covered every bit of exposed skin, and we were burning from head to toe. Still there was nothing they could do to make me quit. When man after man rang The Bell, I no longer feared being next.

By the end there were only eight of the thirty-three who started: one Navy man, the six Coasties from that picture by the front gate, and one of those rolled into the class. We had lost one Coast Guard member who had been with us on that first day of school. The other Coastie who graduated that day was Michael P. Thomas. Weeks earlier he had been dis-enrolled due to pneumonia, but returned to finish with us once he had recovered.

I did not understand how the Navy accomplished their missions with such a high failure rate. I later learned that most Navy training courses, like Aircrew School, had better track records. The glaring exception is SEAL Selection Training. Even with greater pre-screening than Rescue Swimmer School, SEAL training continues to have the highest attrition rate. In all cases though I realized the Navy could throw an endless supply of personnel at a job, like being a rescue swimmer, because they had plenty of conscripted volunteers.

The fear of death at the hands of our Navy trainers was not unfounded. On 2 March 1988, four months after I graduated, five Rescue Swimmer School instructors were involved in the death of 19-year-old Lee William Mirecki.

Lee joined the Navy in October 1987; he dreamed of becoming a naval aviator.

Lee was dis-enrolled from his first rescue swimmer class one month before his death. The Navy was going to revoke his flight status as an aircrewman if he failed to complete the rescue swimmer school. It was the standard practice at the time. He was evaluated by a clinical psychologist and found unfit to continue this type of training. But through an error in procedures he was released by a flight surgeon and elected to try again, despite not having overcome the fear that kept him from passing escape-and-release drills.

During the usual game of Sharks and Daisies the instructors had singled out Lee because of his inability to complete the drills. They ordered the other 26 students from the pool, told them to turn their backs on their classmate, and directed them to sing the national anthem while several instructors trained Lee.

Lee panicked as one after another instructor played victim and wrapped his arms around Lee's head. They repeated the drills until Lee jumped from the pool screaming, "D.O.R. D.O.R.," for Drop on Request, the term used by Navy members to stop training when they felt too tired or afraid to continue. He was crying and screaming as he clung to the metal racks used to hang flight suits. When the lead instructor ordered the others to get him off the rack and back into the pool, it took three men to pry his hands and fingers from the bars.

Once back in the pool Lee struggled loose from their clawing arms, grasped the rope separating the deep end from the shallow, and held on, fearing for his life, but he was again pulled free and taken underwater. His classmates, still with their backs turned, reported hearing splashing and yelling. They turned to see Lee's limp, blue body being pulled from the water. Lee had been Smurfed.

Although the instructors immediately started CPR in an attempt to revive him, all efforts to save Lee's life failed. He died in the ambulance on the way to the emergency room.

Did Lee, as rumors had it, confront the instructors and ask them, "Don't let me quit no matter what I say in the pool." If so, this might explain why the instructors continued even after Lee called D.O.R. If in fact Lee made this request and the instructors honored it, they would have gone against Navy policy. Unfortunately, some of the events surrounding Lee's death will never be known.

The official autopsy reported his death as an accidental drowning. One of the Navy instructors reported to the Lee's sister, "Nothing out of the ordinary happened the day Lee died."

A couple of weeks afterwards, Lee's sister, Lynn Johansen, received several anonymous phone calls from his classmates.

"Lee didn't have to die," each told her in his own way.

Lynn, with help from her husband, Larry Johansen, pressured the Navy to reopen the investigation into her brother's death.

The Navy's Article 32 investigation, the equivalent to a grand jury probe, found that the five instructors "by culpable negligence did unlawfully kill Lee Mirecki by wrongfully and repeatedly forcing Mirecki to continue with a life-saving drill." They were charged with involuntary manslaughter.

One of the lawyers for the defense argued that the Navy set the instructors up for failure and was itself to blame for Lee's death: "The Navy trained them to train in that fashion and told them their instruction techniques were good."

As I look back on the school I agree with the original statement issued by the Navy that nothing out of the ordinary happened that day. The notable exception was that Lee couldn't be brought back from the edge of death.

CHAPTER 4

The First One

I was assigned to the Big Easy from December 1987 to February 1991. A budget crunch in the late 1980's had halted implementation of the swimmer program during 1989. At New Orleans my first leading chief, a crusty old bastard who had been promoted to master chief long before written exams existed, badgered me about the Coast Guard not needing swimmers. He even said during that 1989 lull that I might as well give it up, because rescue swimmers would never be used. For a while I thought he was right.

While his chiding was discouraging, it motivated me. With no control over the timetable, I decided to do something useful.

I became qualified as a flight mechanic and stood duty in that capacity until the time came when I could use my swimmer skills. To that point during my tenure in the service I had participated in many rescues, some as a small-boat crewman, others as an EMT on helicopters, yet I always felt like a small part of someone else's efforts. While acting as a flight mechanic I even received a commendation medal for a rescue I took part in during Hurricane Chantal the summer of '89.

Chantal was a Category One storm that squeaked its way through the Gulf of Mexico. A 300-foot research barge dragging several miles of seismic cable and being towed by two 110-foot seagoing tugs was caught at sea as the storm passed. Looking for deposits of oil, the crew did not have time to reel in the cable before the storm was upon them. Zane Sprey, a crewman, was thrown from the helicopter pad atop the main structure of the barge as he attempted to secure some loose gear. His shipmates treated his injuries but decided to call the

Coast Guard when they suspected he might be bleeding internally. He also suffered a broken collarbone and was in a great deal of pain.

I had duty the night that call came in. My pilot was Lt. Daniel Svensson, with co-pilot Gerry Wilson, and because I was both an EMT and a flight mechanic, I was the only crewman.

Svensson never pulled into a hover, having to maintain about 70 knots of forward airspeed to keep us over the top of the barge. We completed a litter hoist from the same platform where, hours earlier, Zane had been injured. The seas were running about 60 feet, and as the barge plowed up the face of one wave and through the middle of the next, it was buried in green water with each wave. They covered the landing platform as the ship burst through them, forcing us to hoist to it versus landing on it. We had to time the hoist perfectly to avoid losing the patient in a passing wave.

Months later the Eighth District admiral leaned close to my ear as he pinned on my medal for this rescue and said, "There is a fine line between bravery and stupidity. Success and failure are the difference between the two." I knew he was right

Yet despite my success to date, because I had not yet used my hard-won skills as a swimmer I felt like I was a bench warmer on the sidelines. By now, however, I had won over my skeptical master chief who, because he was a flight mechanic and never used a rescue swimmer, considered swimmers useless. With this qualification under my belt he saw me as a useful member of the team and thought that in time I would forget all about being a rescue swimmer.

My first rescue as a swimmer was also the first time Air Station New Orleans ever used a swimmer. It was not an epic battle of physical prowess against the forces of nature; rather, Death almost had me—again. In my case the only reason I am alive to tell the tale is because of a woman named Joy Freeman.

In my world there is no one of greater importance than flight mechanics, our hoist operators during a rescue. They are our lifelines and our only hope for escaping the hell that we enter. The benign-sounding job description is misleading, to say the least. Not only are our flight mechanics responsible for hoisting, they give conning commands to the pilot while doing so, maneuvering the rescue device to us in the worst of storms. They often act as the eyes for a pilot unable to see the target below, and they care for the aircraft while away from the home unit. No rescue swimmer has ever rescued anyone without a flight mechanic, but they have saved countless souls without us.

When we dangle below an aircraft on a ¼" thick cable above a pitching deck, we live and die by the expertise of the person on the hoist control. One wrong move or hoist-control input and a swimmer's thighbones could be shoved through his mid-section. I learned early in my career how important a good flight mechanic can be to my survival.

On 25 March 1990 I was flying as part of the crew of HH-65 helicopter out of Air Station New Orleans, scouring Lake Pontchartrain for an overdue runabout motorboat with three persons on board. Before this search operation no crews from our station had yet deployed a rescue swimmer to the water during a rescue.

The aircraft commander was Lt. Flanner, a quiet, capable, good-natured fellow. The co-pilot, Ltjg. Jackson, earned his nickname, "Action Jackson," while serving in the Air Force. The flight mechanic was Aviation Machinist Mate [AM] Third Class Joy Freeman. Short, with dark hair, she was known as an extremely hard worker who could hold her own, be it knowledge or drink, with any man on the hangar deck.

We flew the back-and-forth search pattern until, on the fourth leg, I spotted a man in the water frantically waving his arms. My heart skipped a beat and I rose an inch or two from my seat.

I gave the person's position in relation to the aircraft, "Person in the water, eight o'clock, left turn."

"Roger, have him in sight,"

The wind barely created a ripple on Lake Pontchartrain, which, though large, was calm that morning. Flanner settled the helicopter into a hover over and off to the side of the man. He could clearly see the survivor's pale skin color and deduced from the lack of motion and the estimated time of 24 hours spent in the water that the man was hypothermic. The water temperature was around 70 degrees, cold enough to cause death with extended exposure. The man was wearing no life jacket and little clothing. He had saved himself by tying a boat gas tank and ice chest together and floating between them.

Flanner directed, "Jerry, let's free-fall you and pick this guy up with a basket. We don't want to do more harm than he's already suffered." The helicopter's hurricane-force rotor wash might have been enough to finish him, and Flanner did not want to risk it. "Do you mind getting wet?"

I had been living for this moment for years, ready to jump out of my skin at the chance. I did a quick evaluation of the conditions and figured this to be a low-risk rescue, by the numbers.

"Hell no, I don't mind."

The manuals that provide guidance for aircrews spell out procedures for deploying a rescue swimmer and we followed them to the letter.

"Complete rescue check list part two for a free-fall deployment of the rescue swimmer," Flanner ordered.

Joy stoically responded, "Roger, bringing swimmer to the door."

"Roger, go on hot mike and conn me in."

"On hot mike, have target in sight, forward and right fifty feet… forward and right forty feet… forward and right thirty feet…hold position," Joy commanded.

Flanner flew the aircraft with a light touch, based upon Joy's input, then said, "Standby to deploy swimmer."

"Roger, checking swimmer," she said and slapped my chest. I flipped the hinged buckle and released the gunner's belt, the last piece of gear attaching me to the airframe. I threw the belt backward and gave Joy my trademark two thumbs up, though only one is required.

"Swimmer's ready."

"Deploy the swimmer," Flanner ordered.

Joy tapped my right shoulder three times. After one last look I heaved myself from the deck of the helicopter and shoved off into the air. I hit the water like a 130 pound boulder and sprinted to the survivor. As we suspected, he was hypothermic and delirious.

"Hey man, I can't leave my stuff," he slurred, more worried about whether we were going to take the ice chest and gas can than if he was going to live.

"I'll bring it with me when they pick me up, but you need to let go."

I spun around to face Joy and gave her a thumbs up, ready for the basket. Nothing happened. I gave the signal again, still nothing. She was glancing at me, then turned her focus toward the rear of the aircraft. I couldn't draw her attention by shouting, so I had to wait until whatever was distracting her was gone. In the next instant Joy stood and began to wave her arms over her head, then point at me. I turned to see what had her so captivated. A big yellow cigarette boat, used for offshore racing, was skirting across the surface headed straight for us. Her waving arms did little to deter its operator from muscling his craft in our direction. Joy was desperate; in seconds we would be dead. I knew she was excitedly explaining to Flanner what was happening, because he pitched the hovering aircraft's blades toward the approaching boat. Finally the driver understood. He yanked back on the throttles and came to a coasting stop 40 yards from my head.

This was my first water rescue and would have been my last had it not been for a flight mechanic who was as sharp as a razor.

Joy was the first in a long line of flight mechanics who made sure I would live another day. Every rescue is a team effort, and the fact that the Coast Guard has never lost a rescue swimmer, except as part of an aircrew that died as a result of an aircraft crash, is testimony to the professionalism and expertise of all Coast Guard flight mechanics, along with all the other members of their teams.

As my crew hovered nearby, several more boats converged upon my survivor and me. Flanner decided it was too dangerous to hover near the boats and began a slow circle around us, calling a sheriff's rescue boat over to assist. The deputies cleared the helpful bystanders and took charge of the survivor, offering to run him to the hospital so we might continue the search for the other two missing men. I accepted their offer, relayed this to Flanner, and jumped back into the lake as the deputy departed, and within minutes I was hoisted back into the helicopter.

We searched without finding the other missing men. For the next several days the Coast Guard had small boats and aircraft scouring the lake and did not find them. About a week later several fishermen found their bodies.

So in that instance I was one for three and not off to an auspicious start. I questioned whether death could be defeated. Was my training sufficient, did I lack some physical ability, was I motivated enough? The answers I wanted did not come to me.

This was the first rescue in which I was able to use my skills as a trained swimmer, but it was not my first rescue ever. My own internal question of whether I was willing to risk everything to save another person was answered every time I recalled my very first one.

My first rescue happened during the summer of 1976. The dog days sweltered under the relentless August sun, overbearing to anyone not accustomed to it. But this blond 10 year-old, darkly tanned Florida boy spent his days at the local swimming pool and hadn't noticed. By 5:00 PM on the last day of the month, my skin wrinkled as a prune, I climbed from the shallow end and walked to the bleachers. After toweling off and slipping on cutoff shorts, a dry shirt, tennis shoes, and socks I glanced around and retrieved my wad of $1 bills from their hiding place under the bleacher bench. I stuffed the dollars into my pocket and slung my towel over both shoulders. It felt good to be somewhat dry after being wet most of the day. The swim trunks soaked through the shorts a little, but otherwise I was comfortable for the bike ride home.

The pool deck was empty, but I remembered exactly where Sara had sunbathed for several hours. Sara was my dream girl, with dark flowing hair and bright smiling eyes. I was walking by her empty chair along the empty pool deck when it happened. The splashing was urgent and near. I looked toward the swimming lanes to see a boy about five years old crossing the pool side to side. Two lanes from the ledge he stopped and began flailing. He was trying to scream, but no sound came from his open mouth. The look of pure terror on his face told me that this was no childish prank or horseplay. I knelt down, leaned out over the water, and extended my arm toward him while holding my towel with my other hand to keep it dry.

"You can reach it, kid, just grab my hand," I commanded impatiently, when suddenly, I felt a swift kick in the ass. I sailed through the air, landing on my face, belly-flopping right next to the kid. The water was deeper than I was tall, but I grabbed the boy anyway. I had been swimming competitively since age five and was as fast as a shark—swimming fully clothed was no problem. With the boy in a cross-chest drag, I turned for the edge. The lifeguard had heard my splash, saw the life-or-death struggle, and was a blur of motion. He covered the 30 yards from his lifeguard stand and was upon us in less than three seconds. I had never seen a person move that fast and gladly released my charge to him, ready to rip someone else limb from limb. But who? The pool deck was still empty. Climbing from the water I looked around and saw no one. Scanning the entire pool area, the snack stand, and both bathrooms, I found no other living creature. The only people there were the three of us involved in this incident.

This save almost didn't happen. My hesitation could have cost this boy his life. This incident has stuck with me through the years, but I have only shared it with two other people before now. I feared being ridiculed, disbelieved. One of the two I told it to said it was God that had kicked me. The other said it was either my over active 10-year old imagination, or my subconscious mind forcing me to act when my conscious mind refused to do so. The story is true, but I will let you decide the source of the kick.

Later in my life, as I sat in the door of a hovering helicopter, 20,000 pounds of complex machine held in the air by several thousand thundering horses, the blades pounding the air into submission, I sometimes thought back to that summer day. It is a quick passing thought: "Don't hesitate." When in my future life the rotor spray was so intense at water level that it turned the air into unbreatheable stinging needles, when waves climbed to the height of tall buildings destroying all life in their grasp, when the black of night hid the dangers that might have caused some to pause, I refused to hesitate. Each time I felt those three taps on my shoulder, I hurled my body into the air, on my way to my next rescue, ever aware that I no longer needed a swift kick in the ass.

CHAPTER 5

The Stan Team

I had joined the Coast Guard during a time of transition; rescue swimmers were new, unproven and often unwanted. I was initially sent to New Orleans because Master Chief Larry Farmer, the father of the swimmer program, was scheduled to bring swimmers on line at that unit. That did not happen right away. (For a behind-the-scenes look at beginnings of the Coast Guard's rescue swimmer program, read Martha LaGuardia-Kotite's book *So Others May Live*).

Besides becoming qualified as a flight mechanic and quelling the grumbling of my command master chief I quietly researched the New Orleans search-and-rescue case files for incidents where a life could have been saved had we had swimmers. I routed a letter with a summary of my findings through my chain of command to Farmer, trying to convince him of the need for swimmers at my unit. I was naïve to think Farmer controlled the budget and implementation process. But my initiative to become qualified as a flight mechanic and pursue this research led him to invite me to join the Standardization Team. I was transferred to Mobile, Alabama, in February 1991.

The Standardization Team (Stan Team) was the research and development branch, enforcer of standards for all Coast Guard rescue swimmers. Already on the team when I arrived were ASM1 Jeff Tunks, ASM1 Scott Dyer, ASM1 Jim Sherman, and, of course, Master Chief Larry Farmer.

At the time of my posting I was arrogant and full of myself, sure they had invited me to join because they recognized my skills. I could not have been more wrong. Joining the Stan Team was, for me, like going to grad school. Sure, I had the basic skills required of any rescue swimmer and had even enjoyed some successes. But I lacked so much more than I knew.

Enamored at serving with the giants of the rescue swimmer world, I was hoping to be included among their ranks. Farmer, especially renowned for his gruff style and intimidating physical presence, had been in the battle for life seemingly forever. On 31 July 1974 he and a co-worker were working in the upholstery shop in Elizabeth City on an aircraft discrepancy. The shop was part of a large complex of buildings lining the runways, and during takeoff a Navy Orion P-3 experienced a mechanical malfunction and crashed into the shop where they were working. Farmer was thrown to the deck by a giant explosion, and what was left of the aircraft burst into flames. The shop was demolished and choked with smoke, burning jet fuel pooled outward, and toxic fumes filled the air as Farmer immediately began to search for his coworker in the debris, a second explosion threw him across the room. Instead of running he got up and continued to search, eventually finding his friend badly injured and unable to move. Farmer stayed by his side until rescue crews arrived, then assisted with the removal of his friend. Even when this was done, Farmer did not run, but opted to stay and help fight the fire.

For his actions that day he was awarded the Coast Guard Medal, one of the highest medals the Coast Guard can bestow, usually reserved for the most senior Coast Guard members. His fearlessness was legendary.

He was qualified in every type of rotor-winged aircraft, qualified drop master on C-130s, and as a flight mechanic on H-3 helicopters. He wrote the qualification syllabus for all rescue swimmers on all aircraft and the first *Rescue Swimmer Procedures Manual*. Most of his work was modeled on the Navy rescue swimmer program, but he recognized the differences between the Navy's training and the Coast Guard's missions. His work was new. He was blazing a trail for the rest of us to follow.

When he entered the office each morning he moved his broad shoulders as if bulldozing the air out of his path and often tilted his bald gleaming head forward to glare in my direction. His style was one of contradiction; he often solicited new ideas from those around him, yet once his decision was made it was as if the word of God had been handed down.

One of the first lessons I learned from him was the importance of structure to the accomplishment of the mission. The mission came before personal feelings and beliefs. If someone senior to gave him an order, Farmer behaved as if that order had come directly from him, even if he strongly disagreed.

I feared him, but I feared disappointing him more. During my first few days at my new job, Farmer's scowl landed on me more than once as he studied my 140-pound frame. He never voiced his doubts about my abilities aloud, but shortly after I arrived he took me on a swimmer flight to see for himself. I did not know it was a test, but it was. Could I handle my own in the water? That was his only question.

During the flight Farmer explained that I was to react exactly as I would during an actual rescue. Once we were in a hover over the tepid waters of Mobile Bay, he hurled himself into the brown water and swam away with long powerful strokes. I did not hesitate when the flight mechanic tapped me on my right shoulder. I too flung my body into the air and sprinted towards Farmer as soon as I landed. I executed a perfect quick reverse approach, placed my arms across his massive chest, and signaled for a basket pickup. He squirmed and thrashed, trying to break my grip as he played the part of a panicked survivor, all to no avail. In a minute he was on his way up. We repeated the process at least half a dozen times with different rescue methods, but always with the same result.

"Ok, he's good to go," Farmer said to Dyer when we were back in the office the next morning. I had passed Part One of Farmer's litmus test. Part Two was on my desk.

The swimmers in Savannah, Georgia, had a rash of concern about their extreme exposure to jellyfish. During the summer, they said, it was too hot to wear the double-layered long wet suit, and the shorty wet suit left too much skin exposed. Even though I was fairly inexperienced, I realized they had a legitimate complaint. The thick suit would likely cause them to suffer some degree of heat exhaustion, and if, while wearing the short suit, they had an allergic reaction to jellyfish stings, they could die. "How would you solve that problem, Jerry?" was the only direction Farmer gave.

The solution seemed simple enough; they needed a long, thin, wet suit. I started with this thought and researched what already existed to protect recreational divers and found numerous dive skins and wet suits on the open market. I ordered two or three of each type of suit, so each member of the team could test them during flights. At this early stage of R and D, we did not worry about military specifications (Mil Specs) contracts or any other major details. We just wanted to know what worked and what didn't.

The Aviation Training Center in Mobile is the unit where our pilots are trained to fly Coast Guard aircraft and use our procedures. This is their first stop after they complete standardized military aviation school. Hence we had many opportunities there to test new gear and procedures. It was on one of these routine flights that I chose to try a new 2-millimeter thick wet suit that happened to be hot pink. If this suit worked, we intended to specify in the contract all aspects of the suit's makeup, including the color.

The flight was smooth sailing through multiple deployments, and I was pleased that I could rotate my arms freely, the suit did not chafe and it was comfortable in both hot air and warm water. I did not feel overheated. Toward the end of the flight, late in the afternoon, we received a call from the Coast Guard small-boat station in Mobile requesting us to divert to an overturned boat in the mouth of the bay with multiple persons in the water.

My aircraft commander responded, "Roger that, we're on our way." The air station in New Orleans was responsible for Mobile Bay and east to Panama City. Technically this was their case because the Mobile-based training center does not maintain a rescue helicopter in ready status. But that did not deter us.

Within minutes we were hovering near a Coast Guard 41-foot boat that had hauled all the survivors aboard. They were performing CPR on a man of about 50.

"Request immediate medivac," the coxswain called over the radio when he saw us arrive overhead.

Within minutes I was pumping the chest and ventilating an unconscious and unresponsive man. Sweat poured off my body, stinging my eyes. The one-way valve mask I was using was slippery in my hands. When the man vomited seawater, I rolled him to his side to clear his airway. I had no EMT kit onboard, only a small pocket mask I kept in my swimmer bag. I would have liked to have used a plastic airway to maintain an open passage down his throat. Instead, I had to reposition his head every time I attempted ventilations. It would be years before the automatic defibrillator would become standard EMT gear—another piece of gear, that, in hindsight, I wish I had had. Since that day, I have never again flown without an EMT kit, regardless of the mission.

The transport time to the hospital was 15 minutes. I realized that my CPR was barely exchanging air, but by the time we had landed his lips were no longer blue. As the flight mechanic and I unloaded the patient onto a gurney, a petite flight nurse jumped onto the man's supine body and began compressions while I continued with ventilations. I was completely oblivious to the stares of bystanders as I entered the hospital in my hot pink wet suit. I had so much sweat in my eyes the entire scene was a blur. After the attending doctors took over, I turned to leave when I was stopped in the hall.

"You need to sit, you're pale as a ghost," the flight nurse told me as I walked down the hall, head hung low. Even though I had done my best I was sure my patient was dead, this was a battle I had lost. But the nurse was smiling at the sight of me, despite the grave nature of our business.

So the suit worked well in the most stressful test possible, where, I believe a thicker wet suit would have kept me in the hospital with heat exhaustion. As it was, I just needed some water to replace the fluids I had lost. The suit passed with flying colors (literally). Within a couple of months we issued the first, optional, mil-spec defined, jellyfish suit for all rescue swimmers assigned to southern units, in black and red. And, I had passed Farmer's second test.

I was assigned various missions under the close supervision of the other swimmers in the office: visiting air stations on standardization visits, researching new equipment and procedures. I was learning to think outside the dogmatic regulations that guided to our profession. The mission was always first, the "how" was open to innovation.

When I joined the team, Farmer was near the end of his tour and close to accomplishing his mission of bringing rescue swimmers to Coast Guard aviation. The last unit to be brought online was Air Station Chicago, and Farmer invited me to join him. I was excited and nervous beyond words. In July 1991, after a week of ground training, flying, and lectures, Farmer had finally accomplished the insurmountable. There were no parades, or awards ceremonies, not even a pat on his back. We just sat in the hotel bar and drank a beer. Awestruck, I did not know what to say, so I said nothing. I never really doubted his ability to accomplish his mission, as all swimmers refuse to fail.

A few months later Farmer transferred to Coast Guard headquarters to the newly created job of Rescue Swimmer Program Manager. His departure and the arrival of Master Chief Darryl Gelakoska ushered in a new era filled with rapid changes for rescue swimmers.

Jeff Tunks was on the Stan Team because he singlehandedly transformed the way pilots and flight mechanics viewed rescue swimmers. Jeff was one of the early pioneers, having become a rescue swimmer shortly after Farmer started the program. His first duty station was in Sitka, Alaska, and like a lot of us he had to endure open hostility. Many aircrew members, especially the aircraft commanders, did not believe swimmers were needed. At my first unit I often remember waiting for an announcement, "Rescue Swimmer Provide," after the blaring of the SAR alarm. If I did not hear those words then the aircraft commander did not want me to go. This was true until Jeff's actions began the slow change of attitude toward swimmers. It started on 11 December 1987 when Jeff rescued Jim and Clint Blades from the deadly Alaskan Sea.

The aircrew had attempted numerous basket hoists, but the weather was too horrendous, violently batting the rescue device through the air, making it uncontrollable. They had run out of options. Finally, as a last resort, the aircraft commander turned to Jeff, "Do you want to go in?"

Jeff had sat in the back of the aircraft watching the events unfold, feeling helpless until that moment. "No problem," he said.

Jeff was successful. The entire team was successful—barely. Jeff was hoisted into and rescued the Blades from 30-foot seas and hammering winds, and survived being slammed into the face of several waves as the aircraft was blown backward during his pickup. He almost did not survive it—almost.

Jeff was awarded a Distinguished Flying Cross with Valor for his efforts, featured in *Readers Digest* and later in Spike Walker's book *Coming Back Alive*. And he had announced the arrival of rescue swimmers to the rest of Coast Guard aviation.

I would have followed Jeff anywhere, and in June of 1992 I got my chance when Gelakoska assigned Jeff and me to work with NASA engineers on escape pod testing in College Station, Texas. The pod was known as the Assured Crew Return Vehicle (ACRV).

Texas A&M University had an indoor wave pool that was 22 feet deep at the sides and 55 feet deep in the center. The capsule was tied to a metal bridge by two enormous bungee cords. The bridge spanned the pool in front of a multi-paddle wave-making machine that dwarfed the wave machines used at commercial wave parks. The waves were broken apart by multiple rows of underwater chain link fence as they approached the back wall. The university used this indoor facility to test models of offshore oilrigs. It was capable of generating waves of up to 8 feet, large enough that the Coast Guard would have turned a 41-foot utility boat back toward shore if it encountered them.

I followed Jeff up the face of a wave toward the bobbing metal casing when he stopped and spun toward me. "You ready?"

"Yeah," I said over the sound of rushing water.

We were looking at 10 feet of vertical metal cylinder. On top, antennas sprouted everywhere. The American flag painted on its side bounced sideways as I circled the pod looking for the black-and-yellow boarding handles. Three engineers playing the part of astronauts were inside.

Jeff was letting me take the lead, gauging my decision-making abilities on this strange new mission. We were in the water, sure, but I had never boarded anything like this before. I grabbed the handle as the wave dropped from underneath the capsule. One second I was in the water; the next I was hanging from the handle in midair. I hauled myself up, turning my right fin sideways and wedging my foot on the first rung. I stooped and removed first one fin, then the other, shifting my foothold as I did so. I tossed the fins onto the top of the pod and climbed upward so Jeff could follow.

We tightly gripped whatever handhold presented itself and worked as a team to breach the secured hatch on the roof. Gravity opened it, pulling the hatch downward, and I peered into the darkness.

"Everybody all right?" I yelled and received moans of differing levels from the three men inside.

Without hesitation I jumped inside the capsule and let my eyes adjust to the dim light from the open hatch. Tunks slid to the opening and waited for my next move. I checked pulses and asked if anyone could talk or move, getting little more than affirmative groans. They were simulating having been in the weightlessness of space so long that they had lost of the strength to move under the weight of atmosphere.

The project manager had engineers, underwater safety divers, photographers, and probably a hundred other workers watching us. They wanted to know how to build a rescuer-friendly escape pod that required no special training to effect a rescue. They invited rescue swimmers and Air Force pararescuemen to this site to test their mock escape pod. The engineers were brave enough to play the incapacitated victims, adding a surreal realism to our practice runs. Where we placed our hands, how we boarded the capsule, whether it was easier to exit the side or the top, how long each rescue took, and probably a thousand of other details were documented at multiple camera angles and by live observers.

The unusual nature of this type of rescue and practicing it under the legendary wing of Jeff Tunks gave me time to ponder the implications. Since my arrival on the Stan Team I had truly stepped outside the stiff regulations drilled into my head as I trained to be a rescue swimmer. I came to embrace a larger view of what it meant to battle for life over untimely death. My original perspective, in which I personified death, remained the same, but there were other ways outside the box to defeat death besides direct confrontation. Everything I did as part of the Stan Team was to prepare others for the fight, giving them the tools to win and broadening my understanding of what it meant to be part of a team.

During this early stage of the program, every time a swimmer was used on a SAR case the unit to which he was assigned was required to send us a message detailing the rescue. Down in our Stan Team office, which was in the back of the shipping warehouse on the training base in Mobile we read each rescue-swimmer message with great interest, gleaning enormous amounts of information.

One of these messages told of a swimmer on the West Coast hoisted to the top of a 400-foot tower to rescue an injured repairman. In another instance a swimmer was lowered through the tree canopy to an injured lumberjack, then climbed a mountain carrying the injured man to a clear hoisting site. As reports like these flowed in to our office from around the country, we became convinced that a swimmer would soon be seriously injured or killed. Because of this, Gelakoska tasked us with solving all the training and equipment deficiencies we could identify. But before we had developed coherent solutions to the myriad challenges the swimmers faced we received the message we had been dreading.

The message flashed across our computer screens, with a videotape of the entire accident to follow. ASM3 Daniel Patrick Chick had fallen off a cliff while attempting to rescue a stranded hiker. Daniel, who for a while went by his abbreviated middle name, Pat, was, at the time of his accident, a recent graduate of Aviation Survivalman School in March of 1990. Not long after his commanding officer awarded him the gold aircrew wings, Pat was proudly standing duty and anticipating the calls that would showcase his special skills.

It's helpful to know the mentality of rescue swimmers, as I feel it played a role in this case. For years I have attempted to identify the shared characteristics of all swimmers, the river that runs through all swimmers' souls. While it's difficult to pinpoint absolutes, there is always the risk of finding an exception. Nevertheless, I comfortably contend rescue swimmers are infused with the following traits: Type A personalities ranging from outgoing to outrageous, the desire to control bad situations and improve the outcome, and the inner drive enabling them to complete physical tasks beyond the normal bounds of human strength. First and foremost, they are unable to comprehend their own failure, no matter the obstacles. Or, as is my case, they fear failure. I had long come to terms with the fact that I would rather die than fail, but I had yet to directly confront that fear.

Master Chief Farmer had hoped we would be the "quiet professionals." But those of us physically and mentally capable of passing the school are usually anything but. We are usually loud and confident.

Forty-five minutes after launching, the helicopter crew found their target clinging to the side of a sheer cliff about 200-feet above the rocky beach. He was still an estimated 100-feet from the top. The aircrew did not know how or why the hiker was perched so precariously. He was frozen with fear and waiting for his rescuers to make the next move.

The aircraft commander, Lcdr Gromlich, asked Pat if he wanted to go get the guy. Pat replied, "OK."

When we communicate verbally, what is said and what is heard can have two completely different meanings. What both parties in the conversation mean might be something else entirely. Pat was relying on the expertise of the others in the aircraft and offered no other options or opinion. Also, it would have been uncharacteristic for him or any swimmer to voice doubts about his ability to succeed.

When Gromlich heard Pat say "OK," he interpreted it as Pat's eagerness to go and his confidence in getting the job done safely. Pat, on the other hand, understood it to mean, "If you think I should go, then I will go." There is still controversy among the crew as to what was said and how they arrived at the decision to put Pat on the cliff.

Pat wished he had spoken up as he hung in the open sky from a steel cable the diameter of a clothesline, 250-feet above the rocky beach.

Downward he went and, much sooner than he was ready, contacted the cliff. He quickly learned it was not the solid surface he had thought, but loose shale. Each time he was slammed into the soft earth, soil and rock slid down the mountain from under his feet. He bounced into the sheer face several times before gaining a solid footing about five feet below the survivor. To Pat it seemed unbelievable that falling rocks had not knocked the man to his death.

It was unusual for a Coast Guard helicopter crew to attempt a cliff side rescue, but even more so to have a scenic overlook a couple hundred yards away. It was about this time that a passing tourist began taking video of the hovering helicopter and the sequence of events, adding commentary to the exciting footage.

Pat wedged his feet into the soil, clamped onto a protruding root, and released the sling. The hook and sling were hoisted back to the helicopter as Pat and the survivor waited on the basket. When the root began to pull free from the ground; Pat looked up and calmly stated to the wide-eyed man, "If you can't get me a better hold of this cliff you'll watch me fall."

The man leaned down and pulled Pat closer, allowing him to grip something a little more solid. Once the immediate danger had passed Pat explained they were going to make this one hoist. He told the survivor they would grab the sides of the basket and climb down the cliff as the flight mechanic paid out slack. They would use the basket to keep from losing footing as they descended.

"OK," the man replied shakily.

On tape the tourist was heard exclaiming to her friend, "That man [stuck on the cliff], put that other man [Pat] in danger." She was referring to the fact that if he had not climbed into a position that required rescue, Pat would not have put himself onto the cliff to rescue him.

Pat sighed with relief as the basket came within reach and he clamped down on the metal rail with all his might. The tape shows the basket swinging away from the mountainside as the survivor grabs it. Unable to maintain his grip or support his entire weight as he lost footing, Pat fell, bouncing off rocks, loosely spinning between slams into the slope, somersaulting numerous times the last 20 to 30 feet. The camera followed with grunting sounds from the narrating tourist as Pat collided with the cliff during his rapid descent. The survivor latched onto the basket like a vise grip, however, and was lowered to the beach below. The helicopter crew believed Pat was dead but completed the rescue as they had briefed.

Two people watching the rescue from the beach are shown sprinting to the fallen swimmer as the tourist wraps up her commentary with, "Oh my God! Oh my God!"

Amazingly, Pat survived his fall and was loaded by his own aircrew into the helicopter and transported to a local hospital. After a CAT scan and x-rays Pat learned his injuries were not life threatening. He was released from the hospital three days later.

This was our great challenge, to prepare swimmers for rescues beyond the water. Gelakoska's style of leadership was as different from Farmer's as anyone could imagine. Farmer used position power to direct us toward the organizational goal in a straight line. Gelakoska used personal power to cajole, befriend, and flatter others into working toward his goals.

It fell to Gelakoska to direct the investigation into this accident. The results of his findings led us to develop and implement a new rescue procedure he dubbed Direct Deployment. Additionally, he created the Advanced Rescue Swimmer School (ARRS) in Cape Disappointment, Washington.

Direct Deployment required a swimmer to stay on the hoist hook for the duration of the rescue. We borrowed ideas from the British and Canadians and came up with a few of our own. We also created two new pieces of gear, the quick strop and the seat harness. The quick strop allowed us to snatch and grab a survivor from the water, cliff, or rooftop, while the seat harness supported our weight while holding us in a rappelling position.

The ARRS was more ambitious than the creation of a new rescue procedure. It was Gelakoska's brainchild and, alongside the others on the team, I spent the remainder of my tour working on its creation.

ARRS was to teach rescue swimmers, pilots, and flight mechanics how to complete a very wide variety of rescues not taught in our basic rescue-swimmer training. It focused on helicopter rescues to mountains, swift water, caves, heavy surf, buildings (or any vertical surface), and survival at sea. Gelakoska used all his wiles and connections, calling in every favor to create this school.

CHAPTER 6

Sunset Limited

While helping Gelakoska create these new methods of rescue might seem the crowning achievement of my time in Mobile, it really was Gelakoska's finest moment. I experienced a much more internal realization that I consider my greatest achievement. The train wreck of Amtrak's *Sunset Limited* was the event that marked my most significant growth and was what I remember most about my tour in Mobile.

On Thursday 23 September 1993 the captain of a tugboat pushing a barge took a wrong turn as he transited north on the Mobile River, an unfamiliar course that took him up a waterway known as Little Bayou Canot. He piloted the barge into a rail bridge. The impact dislodged the track from its bed and cracked several pilings, in the dark of night just minutes before Amtrak's Miami-bound high-speed train crossed the bridge. At approximately 2:47 AM the train engine bolted from the trestle and slammed into the mud on the far bank of the small river, taking several passenger cars into the water with it.

Most of the passengers were asleep when the train derailed, so was I. A survivor reported everything went black, the rail car thumped violently, and they were in the water.

When my bedside phone rang I did not look at the clock, merely answered sleepily, "What?" I thought it was a wrong number, because I had not been awakened in the middle of the night to respond to a SAR case for a couple of years.

"Oh, man, there has been a train wreck! We need you to come in!" the anonymous voice on the other end said. I dropped the phone and was running by the time I had reached the front door. I lived only four miles from the base and was there in less than two minutes. I slid to a stop in the parking lot, grabbed my swimmer gear, and ran for the tarmac.

In the bayou life and death were raging against one another. Every type of emergency agency had sent everybody they could contact. Civilians, Coasties, sheriff's deputies, firefighters, and numerous others were pulling people from the water.

The train was burning with thick black flames, filling the air with noxious fumes. The sleeping cars were jumbled in the water at all angles, some jutting up, others completely submerged.

I don't remember the crew I flew with that night, but I do recall dropping down to land our HH-65 on the deck of a nearby barge. The rescuers had brought several injured survivors to the barge whom we were to fly to the hospital. As soon as the helicopter settled onto the landing gear I was scooting toward the open door.

"Going off ICS, exiting the aircraft," I told my aircraft commander. I waited on confirmation, then was out. I ran to the nearest patients lying on the rear of the barge. Several people were talking to me, giving accounts of their injuries and other information. I quickly knelt next to a patient, checked pulse and asked if she was all right, then the next, then the next. From two of the first five I came to I got a slurred response and no response. I hustled back to the helicopter and attached my helmet.

"I've got two that need to go right now. Why don't I give you the first one, have you guys call another helo down, and I'll load the second on it. That will give me time to assess all the patients as they come aboard," I said over the ICS.

Within two minutes of our landing, my first patient was strapped to a backboard, loaded in the aircraft, and on her way. The second helicopter was dropping down as soon as the first one had tilted away.

In about fifteen minutes I had supervised the medical evacuation of seven patients and was waiting on more to be brought to the barge. For several tense moments I thought I was about to be overwhelmed, but the new patients never showed up. There were so many people assisting in the rescue that most of the survivors had been whisked away.

By sunrise the pace of the rescue had slowed, and several other swimmers had joined me on the barge. We all had been bracing for the worst. Then the bodies started to arrive, shuttled to us so that the small boats involved in the recovery could carry more of the dead. By this time in my short career I had witnessed much death, come close to facing my own demise many times, and seen death in others in various forms. I had given much thought over the years to how to defeat death and questioned whether death could be beaten. I also considered any rescue in which I failed a professional and personal defeat.

But as I stood on that barge, with a pasty film of smoke on the roof of my mouth, looking at the limp limbs and waxy skin of the dead, I had an awakening. I could not have arrived at this enlightenment without having followed the path I had chosen. The bodies being brought to the barge did not represent a personal defeat. My collective storehouse of experiences made me realize that dying was a natural part of life and that my perception of life and death as opposites was false. In fact they are really just different points along the same journey. Death was no more malicious than birth. I wondered, "Have I stopped valuing life?" and eventually decided, "No, life is still worth the struggle." With this new knowledge I accepted the reality that death was not to be feared.

I also realized that a swimmer who does not fear death is capable of almost anything, once the urge to withhold effort during a rescue as an act of self-preservation is removed.

My aircraft commander called over the radio, breaking up my thoughts, "Jerry, are you ready to be picked up?" I looked at the bodies being laid on the deck, "Yes sir, I'm ready."

As the helicopter lifted off I watched the bodies get smaller. My mind reeled from my new insight. If death was not this great evil I had been railing against all these years, then what did I fear? What drove me? With galvanizing clarity it dawned: I feared failure. And if I failed, and death was the result, then that was the greatest failure I could experience. For all this new understanding of myself, I knew I had not yet faced this fear and conquered it. At that moment a great weight descended onto my shoulders.

Members of all branches of the military are routinely transferred in order to meet the needs of the service, and in 1994 I was transferred to Coast Guard Air Station Clearwater. During my tour in

Mobile I had broadened my understanding of myself and of the rescue-swimmer profession. I also had learned one other thing: I hate sitting on the sidelines. I was glad to be back in the action.

CHAPTER 7

Inspiration

As I related my stories through the years I have been asked many times who inspired me to become the man I am. The boy I was bore little resemblance to the man I have become, mostly through the equal influences of my two very different grandfathers.

My grandmother, Joyce, married Talmadge Hendry when my father was five. While not a blood relative, Talmadge was the only grandfather (on my dad's side) that I ever knew. He was a World War II veteran turned welder who worked long hours. When I was old enough to understand what she was showing me, my grandmother brought out his medals from their hiding place and showed them to me—a Purple Heart and Silver Star, along with several others. I asked how he got them but was told only in the vaguest terms about the islands in the Pacific. He was the sergeant of his platoon, and I can remember hearing him phone ordering flowers in the shape of his unit patch for the funerals of his men as they passed away through the years. He was a gruff man who smoked too much, laughed a lot and loved us grandkids more than life itself. An outdoorsman who rarely shot game, he dreamed of the day he could go to his hunting camp at the beginning of the season and stay until the end.

The greatest lesson I learned from him was how to love unconditionally. To him nothing was more important than taking care of his adopted son David, who was blind and deaf. He freely and gladly gave up his dreams in order to care for David during the last thirty years of his life. Later in my life as I met some important people and people who thought they were important, I realized they cast small shadows compared to a blue-collar welder from central Florida.

Ed Watkins, my mom's father, was a keen businessman who saw opportunities that others overlooked. Throughout his life he took risks and reaped both rewards and setbacks. He was a farmer, owned a tractor dealership, had a timber operation in South America, and sold heavy equipment. He dabbled in real estate and played the stock market. And he too was an avid sportsman.

He would often pack up and leave for another outdoor adventure on the spur of a moment. My grandmother Marcia kept the home running smoothly between his jaunts to the Keys, the Everglades, and Colorado or wherever he was headed. He knew Indian trackers in the Everglades, held a pistol on would-be bandits, built and rode swamp buggies, and generally had a contagious thirst for adventure. And I caught it.

Those who knew me as a child and young man would not have believed me capable of the things I have related in this book. I wore my emotions on my sleeve and was far from a stellar athlete. I gave up my competitive swimming before high school, after which all my sporting activities revolved around hunting and fishing. Even today when I return to my home town I find that those who knew me years ago still define me by their memories of my youthful stupidity.

Whenever I can, I tell my two daughters, Samantha and Cheyenne, and other impressionable young relatives stories of our family's colorful history, for I know they cannot weather the storms of life or reach their chosen destination without knowing where they started.

It was these two men who gave me a home port from which I launched my own life. While my story is different from theirs, it shares some similarities. My love of the outdoors borders on obsession, I'm always seeking new adventures, love my family, and have dabbled successfully in real estate. And I have added a new dimension to my life through expression of my artistic urges. I draw and write and build things and generally am good at seeing what could be versus what is.

Both grandfathers have passed away. At Talmadge's funeral an American flag draped coffin, and a red hourglass-shaped flower display sat nearby, sent by the few remaining survivors of his old Army unit.

That flag, now tightly folded into a triangle, sits above my fireplace today. Above it, on a couple of cypress knees serving as holders, I keep a vintage Remington double-barrel shotgun that belonged to Ed. These two powerful symbols of both men watch over me every day, and I hope I have made both my grandfathers proud.

The stories of my two grandfathers might suggest I had a perfect foundation and led a trouble-free life—not so. Like everyone else I suffer with my own demons, weaknesses, and mistakes. I struggle every day, and while the grandfathers were my greatest childhood influences, it is my wife Brianne who inspires me as an adult. For Brianne, being married to me has been more challenging than any rescue I have ever participated in. For her the flight never ends and the case is never over. I am proud to acknowledge the strength of the woman who loves me.

We met on a commercial flight to North Bend, Oregon, me for a standardization check of the swimmers at the air station in North Bend, her to visit her mom. At the time she lived in Los Angeles, I lived in Mobile. If she had not worked for an airline, I doubt we would have been able to make the long-distant relationship work. Years later after we married she moved without complaint wherever the Coast Guard transferred me.

Brianne understands my need to live on the edge, for she too has known the adrenaline rush of rescue work, first as a volunteer firefighter, then later as a paid firefighter. Never did she complain about the risks I accepted, nor the long and unusual hours I worked. She did not shy away from my retelling of my workday, understanding the life I lived. Today she works as the emergency management director for the county in which we live.

A news anchor once asked me what my wife thought of my dangerous occupation. This question had come up early in our marriage, and her response was one that made me smile. I knew she understood.

"The Coast Guard better not show up at my door to tell me he's dead unless they have a check in their hands," she said. To some this may seem callous, but to me it meant she knew that I was doing what I loved and that if I died I would want her taken care of. I knew too, that she could have died in her line of work. We understood each other. For us it works.

This connection and mutual understanding of risk also gave me permission to delve into other areas of my life that have nothing to do with the Coast Guard. Our purchase of a timber farm in North Florida was significant, because it meant some sacrifices. We could not buy a big house, as some of my peers did. We were investing in our future at the expense of the present, and like all investments it was far from a sure thing. Fortunately that risk was providing us a place to escape and wind down from the pressures of our professions. We became adept at camping, spending one weekend a month in the forest. We spent nine years cutting down pine trees and building a log cabin with little more than a couple of chainsaws and help from friends and family.

Knowing that Brianne understands and accepts me melded well with my newfound realization in the aftermath of the *Sunset Limited* incident and gave me permission not to hold back. I could do whatever had to be done to do to accomplish the mission, whether that mission was taking financial risk, building a log cabin, or jumping out of helicopters.

CHAPTER 8

Medivacs

During the summer of 1994 the second mass exodus of Cuban rafters put to sea. The first one, known as the Mariel Boat Lift, had taken place in 1980. One of my cousins eventually married a boy who had been rescued at sea that year. As that rarity, a Florida native, I know that our shared history with Cubans and Cuba is so intertwined that we are all like family. I feel a special connection to our Cuban neighbors.

I was on duty that summer day when a boatload of refugees came under fire from Castro's navy as they fled on a 110-foot coastal freighter.

Lcdr Jeff Garden was my aircraft commander. While his imposing frame seemed to block out the sun, he has a pleasant personality that draws people to him. Garden and I had been stationed together in Mobile. He was on the pilots' HH-60J Stan Team, and we traveled together often while completing unit standardization visits. We even flew into the Perfect Storm together, looking for the missing Air Force PJ made famous by Sebastian Junger's book of the same name. We were coincidentally in Cape Cod for one of those visits when that storm roared ashore. We offered our services and spent two days looking, albeit unsuccessfully. Garden and I were again stationed together in Clearwater and I was glad to have him as my aircraft commander.

So many years have passed since that flight to the Keys that the details have blurred. I remember Garden requesting a flight surgeon (we often referred to a flight surgeon as "Doc") and a corpsman accompany us and that the transit from Clearwater to the Florida Straits south of Key West took a couple of hours.

After doc and I were lowered to the deck of a Coast Guard cutter, Garden instructed me to escort the doc to the freighter and assist as required. We jumped into the cutter's rigid-hull inflatable boat and were whisked over the rolling seas. The 5-foot waves did little to the freighter, but they lifted the small boat close enough for us to climb over the gunwale if we timed our scramble with a passing crest. I waited on the bow and grabbed the handrail and stuck a foot in a scupper as the small boat dropped out from beneath me. The doc had never done anything like this before, so it took him a couple of minutes to work up the nerve to try it. I straddled the hard metal rail and grabbed his hand as he tried and failed to find footing, dangling over the side of the ship until I was able to pull him over.

The ship was painted black, with rusty steel showing through, and a large crane sat forward of the super structure, amidships. Bullet holes dotted the crane and superstructure and shatterproof glass had scattered in little square shards all over the deck. I heaved my medical pack off my back and removed my helmet as I worked my way through the refugees down the port side with the doc following closely. Communications were a challenge, as neither of us spoke Spanish, but we found our first patient by following the frantic hand waving. He was inside the galley on a table, bleeding from a gunshot wound to his neck, with blood soaking through the tee shirt another passenger held against his throat. The blood had made the deck slick and was splattered everywhere.

"Doc, if you got this guy, I'll treat the rest and call you if I need you. OK?"

"Go ahead, Jerry."

Doc was opening his medical bag as I left.

"Had to be a nick to the artery to bleed that much. I don't know how he's still alive," I thought as I made my way aft toward the mass of passengers.

I found one man sitting upright against a bulkhead with a bullet wound to his thigh just below his groin. He was grimacing and spouting a string of what sounded like obscenities, sprinkled with Castro's name.

"At least he has a good airway," I thought as I cut away a small section of his pants. His wound was not serious, having just nicked the fleshy part of his muscle. I smiled and nodded, agreeing with his assessment of Castro, as I bandaged his wound.

Another patient was lying on the deck in the next compartment over with a mangled right foot. He screamed as I cut off his tennis shoe and had to be held down by another passenger while I bandaged what remained of his foot. Worried that the fracture might cut an artery and bleed out, I cast his leg, immobilizing it from the knee down with a makeshift splint.

"Jerry!" I heard my name and hurried forward. Doc had performed an emergency tracheotomy and was finishing his patient's bandages as I rushed into the room. I carefully helped place a C collar on our patient.

Doc said as we finished, "We need to get this man to Key West right now."

I grabbed my radio and briefed Garden on our first hoist.

Not knowing how many injured people we had on the ship, the command center in Miami had sent two more helicopters down from Clearwater besides the one I had arrived on. All three aircraft were buzzing overhead waiting for our direction.

I grabbed the hard plastic backboard the cutter's crew had provided and brought it into the galley, then doc and I used the help of bystanders to move our patient over. The corridor was too tight to bring a litter forward, so using hand signals, we enlisted the help of some uninjured passengers to carry our patient forward.

"Cover him with your body as the helo moves in to keep the debris from flying into his face," I told the doc then moved off to receive the litter.

As the rotor wash blasted the ship, glass began flying around as if caught up in a tornado. Within a couple of minutes we had strapped him in the litter and hoisted him to the helicopter. I signaled for the basket, wanting to send the doc with this first patient in case he went into cardiac arrest. While I was hoisting, doc went to look at the other two patients and was just returning as I set the basket on deck.

"Nice job on those other two, they'll be OK for the ride to Key West," he said just before climbing in. I nodded, turned my face toward the sky, and gave a thumbs up.

Once he was inside the helicopter I radioed Garden and urged him to depart. I would hoist the other two in one of the other helicopters buzzing overhead and either meet him in Key West or back at Clearwater. Garden agreed, tilted the nose of the airframe over, and headed toward shore. We finished the medical evacuation of the other two injured men and left the bullet-riddled ship and remaining passengers in the capable hands of the cutter crew.

Later that day, back at Clearwater while restocking my EMT gear bag, I turned the television on to *Headline News* and saw myself on the ship carrying gear and working with patients. The air station's public affairs officer had turned over video of our rescue to the station. I spent the rest of the day watching the loop of film every 30 minutes, as the channel repeated the story. I had enjoyed my tour on the Stan Team, but it felt great to be back in the action. This was where I belonged.

CHAPTER 9

Blood and Guts

Being a rescue swimmer is very much like joining a fraternity, a membership that will last the rest of your life. Among the brotherhood, stories are shared and legends born. During my stint on the Stan Team, my lack of formal writing skills not withstanding, I wrote a few newsletter articles that focused on our new aircrew position. I greatly enjoyed retelling the stories I received in a format that could be read by all aviators. Farmer and Gelakoska allowed me to write these stories as an effective way to showcase our skills.

One experience in particular has stuck with me all these years. When I began writing this book, I called Al Yates (James Alan Yates, Al to his friends) and asked for his permission to use the story of his medivac of 1991. He not only agreed, he took the time to send me a full account of the events of 1 August 1991.

Emergency medical training is as much a part of being a rescue swimmer as are fitness and fearlessness. I have participated in so many medivacs in my career, I have lost count and most other rescue swimmers have participated in just as many. But Al set a new standard on that hot August day.

Al has a deceptively easygoing manner. Like a lot of swimmers, he does not appear to be a man of extraordinary strength, though he definitely possesses it. One might mistake him for an auto mechanic, schoolteacher, or cable man.

An axiom in the Emergency Medical System (EMS) community describes there are three types of patients. One will live regardless of the care received, a non-life threatening injury. The second will die no matter what we do. The third is the one we train for, this person is on the fence. We work hard on every case where our medical skills are needed, but the ones where our actions make a difference bring the most satisfaction.

Early that August morning, with the summer shrimping season in full swing, there were many boats plying the calm waters of the Gulf of Mexico for the little crustaceans. In the Gulf, at any given time fishing and work opportunities abound. More than 30,000 oilrig workers are stationed offshore, and recreational boaters are always abundant.

The hangar in Corpus Christi is nestled next to miles of fish-filled back-bay waters, and to the east lies Padre Island, a popular site for the spring-break crowds.

The weather was clear, warm, and beautiful when the shrill SAR alarm sounded just minutes into Al's 24 hour day, at 8:19 AM.

"Put the ready HH-65 on the line. Medivac of injured crewman off a shrimp boat," The PA announced. Al yanked the phone from its cradle and punched the number to the operations desk.

"What kind of case is it?" he asked excitedly, wanting to know what EMT equipment was needed.

"It looks like a body pickup, Al. You may want to grab a body bag. This guy's guts are sticking out all over the place. He's stuck in some kind of winch."

"Roger that."

Al didn't like the prospect of retrieving a dead body, but he went to the gear locker inside the survival shop inside the hangar and retrieved a green military body bag anyway. While he rummaged for a body bag Al could hear the line crew towing the French-built helicopter outside.

Inside the helicopter workspace was tight. An avionics rack held the collection of navigation and communication black boxes on the left. To the right in the rear was Al's seat, a stiff foam pad strapped to the deck with a green nylon backrest tightly stretched from floor to bulkhead. The space between the rack and Al's seat was about 3 feet across by 8 feet long. Flight crews often had to turn a Stokes litter (a hoist-capable rescue device used to carry patients supine) on its side to fit through the cabin door. Once inside, the swimmer worked in a crouched position, straddling the patient during a bouncing, unstable flight.

Al stripped off his flight suit and slipped into a thin orange neoprene shorty wetsuit. He heaved the sleeves over his shoulders and coaxed the zipper up the front of his torso. Grabbing his swimmer bag, he ran from the hangar into the bright morning sun.

Al guessed he would probably be hoisted to the deck of the boat, though the aircraft commander had not yet made the decision. During this early stage of the rescue swimmer program all swimmers were required to deploy to boats in the same gear they used during water rescues. The Stan Team felt the safety of the swimmer was paramount, and he should be ready to jump overboard at the first sign of trouble.

The pilots burst through the door of the hangar, and once strapped into the airframe sailed through the checklist. The HH-65 truly sounds like it is screaming, and within minutes they were screaming through the air toward their target, for which they had a good position.

Aircraft commander Lt Brian Hudson was known for his expert flying abilities. Crews had great confidence in him. He circled low around the *Kentucky Daughter*, the shrimper with the injured crewman, discussing the possible ways of doing this medivac, all of them involving putting Al put on the boat.

A grizzled voice broke in on Channel Sixteen, "*C Voyager* to the Coast Guard copter."

"Coast Guard copter six five seven six to the *C Voyager*, go ahead captain."

"Roger Coast Guard, I overheard the problem on the radio. We're standing by for any help you might need."

"Thank you captain, we might just take you up on that."

The *C Voyager* was a crew boat used in every facet of offshore oilrig resupply. These boats characteristically sported a huge blunt bow with a large forward pilothouse while the aft portion was low slung and flat.

From the air the deck of the shrimper *Kentucky Daughter* appeared to be covered in loose netting, bulbous floats, and chain and dried seaborne debris in the nets could become shrapnel when hit by the helicopter's rotor wash. This was no good. In contrast, the resupply ship's large deck was clear and offered an easy hoisting target.

Hudson spoke into the mouthpiece of his helmet, "*C Voyager*, from the Coast Guard helo. Captain, I could use your help today. Can we hoist our rescue swimmer to your boat and get you to put him on the *Kentucky Daughter*?"

"Roger that, Coast Guard."

The copilot walked through the safety steps for the crew boat in preparation for the hoist, as Hudson hover-taxied toward the rear of big boat and discussed this new plan with the aircrew. Then he gave the order: "Complete Rescue Checklist part two for a sling deployment of the rescue swimmer."

The flight mechanic, Aviation Machinist Mate Second Class (AD) Bill Munn, responded, "Roger, going on hot mike." While off duty, Bill and Al often shared a few beers, smiles, and stories and on duty the two worked comfortably together.

Al slung the red nylon medical gear pack over his shoulder. With his left hand he grabbed the small bag containing MAST pants, a medical device that looks like inflatable pants with Velcro attachment points along the front. In use they slip over a patient's lower body to the rib cage, and when inflated they push blood toward the heart, counteracting the effects of shock. Later, medical professionals have debated their argued value versus their risk, but at the time of Al's case they were required to be available.

Reportedly the shrimpboat crew had been reeling in wire cable, feeding it onto a drum. Crewman Rennee Valle was aligning the line as it was being reeled aboard, a job he had done many times. He was comfortable guiding the line with his left foot as it glided by, but something had gone terribly wrong.

As Al sat in the open door, hearing only the whine of gears and chopping of air, he had only the vaguest of idea what he might find. The aircrew followed the normal procedures and hoisted Al to the clear deck of the *C Voyager*.

The captain of the *C Voyager* deftly maneuvered his ship along-side and amidships of the shrimper, staying forward of the booms protruding from the fishing boat's sides, yet getting close enough for Al to step up on the hand rail and jump. Al landed with a thump, gave a wave of thanks to the captain of the crew boat, and spun toward the pilothouse of the *Kentucky Daughter*. Windows sur-rounded the wooden structure like so many eyes, and Al's own eyes locked onto the pale ashen face of the ancient captain whose hands gripped the wheel as if of their own accord. As Al walked by the open door down the starboard side, the captain stared straight ahead, refusing to acknowledge Al's presence, for doing so would mean the skipper would have to confront the reality of his crewman's mangled body. The smell of stale fish was overwhelming. Al hurried along the walkway past the wheelhouse toward the aft deck where the business of fishing took place, as evidenced by the mounds of nets interwoven with lead weights and floats.

Al scanned the deck and noted a pudgy Hispanic crewman standing at the stern with his back turned. He was fiddling with some unseen, menial task, avoiding the obvious problem of removing the dead body from the cable drum.

"Man, I don't want to do this," Al thought. He had not yet spoken to either man on the boat, but he understood they wanted nothing to do with this.

Al focused his attention on the winch and drum and saw nothing. He edged toward the drum, taking the first steps of the longest walk of his life. The winch motor still hummed under the strain of electrical impulses yet held deathly still. The hovering helicopter had flown off a short distance to allow Al to work in a relative quiet, punctuated by the steady heartbeat of the boat's diesel engine.

"I'm not touching this guy until you secure the electricity," Al said forcefully to the crewman at the stern. Still not looking at the drum, the deckhand cut power and the humming died.

Al knelt by the drum and peered underneath, inadvertently gagging as he committed the details to memory. The drum, 3 feet in diameter, had attacked Renee's left leg and foot, eating the lower half of his body with rusty steel cable, completing three complete revolutions of the drum before becoming stuck with human bone and flesh. Rennee's left leg was bound and sliced through to the bone by strands of thick steel cable, bringing the man's left foot to within 18 inches from his face. His body was snugly tucked directly under the drum, his right foot and leg pinned squarely between his shoulder blades and the deck. His right foot and leg had been ripped and twisted in the opposite direction to his left leg and torso. The report of guts hanging out was wrong; it was actually the ball socket of his right femur bone jutting out 5-6 inches through his groin.

Al expected more blood. There was plenty covering the cable, part of the drum, and a small section of the deck, but if this man had bled out there should have been more.

"UUUUURAAA," the dead man moaned.

"Holy Shit, THIS GUY'S ALIVE!" Al thought, his mind screaming with the realization.

"Six Five Seven Six, swimmer—he's alive!" Al nearly yelled into the radio he had yanked from the gear pocket of his life vest.

Al slammed the EMT pack to the deck, ripped the zipper open and fumbled for the rubber gloves. Slipping them on with a snap, he spun around and moved in on the victim for a closer examination.

"Roger that, Al. standing by. Just tell us what you need," the crackling voice answered over the radio he had stuffed back in the vest pocket.

Al soaked up vital information, his mind reeling, and ticking off things he needed to do. "OK, his left leg is broken in numerous places, tib-fib, femur, and just about everywhere else. The cable is cinched tight."

Al knelt and firmly asked, "Hey, can you hear me?" Rennee let out a loud moan.

"Let's see, he's in and out of consciousness and breathing. That cable has to be acting like a pair of MAST pants, keeping his blood pressure up, preventing shock and keeping him alive."

"Don't worry buddy, we're going to get you out of this." That much was true, but Al wasn't sure the victim would be alive in the end. There was no response; Rennee had passed out again. But Al knew hearing was one of the last senses to go. Even unconscious this man might be able to cling to his voice for comfort.

Al stood up and chased a fleeting thought from his mind, "This guy would be better off if I just put a bag over his head and ended his life quickly and painlessly." He reached for his radio, gritted his teeth, and set his jaw for the seemingly insurmountable task of saving Rennee's life.

"Seven six, swimmer," Al called. "I don't have the tools to cut this guy out, I'm going to need some help, any ideas?"

Hudson answered, "We called the air station and they have the Naval Air Station Fire Department standing by with the Jaws of Life."

Al looked at the drum again, "No, I don't think that will work. I need a torch of some kind to cut him loose."

"OK, I'll call Ops and see what else they can think of."

"Roger, standing by." Al pocketed the radio and turned back to attend to Rennee. He unzipped the top flap of the soft-sided oxygen kit to reveal a green-and-silver bottle and checked the pressure by cracking open the valve, forcefully blowing any dust from the servicing head. It read slightly less than 2000 PSI, well above the 1500-pound minimum the Coast Guard required, yet not nearly enough for a lengthy stay on the boat. Swiftly he attached the non-rebreather mask to the bottle port and filled the small bag with 100% oxygen. (A non-rebreather mask is made of thin clear plastic and has a small bag attached to the bottom to hold oxygen as it is fed into the cup covering the patient's mouth and nose.) The mask would have to sit cockeyed on the patient's face, but Al slid the elastic over Renee's head anyway, knowing Rennee needed his blood saturated with oxygen. Done with that, Al again pulled the radio from his pocket, sweat dripping from his face, heart racing.

"Seven Six, swimmer."

"Go ahead, Al."

"While we're at it I'll need some more O2 bottles."

"It looks like the air station has launched a second helo with a DC and a cutting torch."(Al knew a DC was a Damage Controlman, and they were all adept at using a cutting torch).

"I'll call them to see if they can bring some bottles."

After a momentary delay the aircraft radioed Al back. "Al, we're going to depart and get those O2 bottles. The second helo should be here any minute. Do you need anything else?"

"I know I need someone to start IVs, maybe the doc or a corpsman."

"I'll see what I can do."

Al was so focused on his patient and the problems at hand, he hardly noticed the salty air or gentle surge of the boat as it eased along through the waves. He addressed the crewman still standing at the stern. "Tell the captain there will be another helo here in a few minutes, and we will need to do another hoist and boat transfer."

The pudgy crewman returned quickly, "The Captain said he will do whatever you need." Dread and sickening fascination mingled on his ashen face as he watched Al work.

Al didn't have to wait long. The second helicopter flared into a hover just minutes after the first aircraft was gone.

Al was grateful to receive a DC's help, as they are usually assigned to Coast Guard cutters. Their specialty is fighting fires, securing bulkheads of sinking ships, and, as the job description implies, controlling damage in all situations. One of their many talents is improvised cutting and welding. The ability to do this while bouncing around on the back of a shrimper slick with fish slime is a special skill.

Al watched the perfectly smooth delivery of the burly DC to the deck of the *C Voyager*. Another hoist landed the tools of the welder's trade, and Al patiently waited for the two ships to pull dangerously close to each other once again. The DC heaved the cutting torch and actylene bottle across the short distance of open sea between the boats, then, stepping onto the rail, crossed the distance himself as if he had done it a thousand times. He followed Al down the starboard rail to the rear of the boat and Renee, where he stared in disbelief and let out a low whistle before beginning the quick process of setting up the torch.

Al was distracted by the high-pitched whine of a second helicopter as it approached the two boats. He turned skyward to see the second aircraft circling wide, and as if on queue, the radio jumped to life, "Swimmer from the two nine."

"Two nine, swimmer, go ahead."

"We've got Doc Freming on board, the Navy flight surgeon. We will be hoisting him to the *C Voyager* in just a second."

Al breathed a sigh of relief.

Lt Brett Freming was green around the gills from the smooth rolling motion of the boat in the 2-foot swells. Al reached out and helped him across, and, with a quick wave of thanks to the crew of the *C Voyager,* began leading the way aft.

The DC stood next to the drum, unlit torch in his hand, waiting. Al knelt down and checked the oxygen pressure, felt Rennee's neck for a pulse, and was rewarded with a weak, rapid beat. Not a good beat but not missing either. Al half expected the Doc to take over the rescue and extraction, but to Al's surprise he asked, "What do you think, Al?"

"I think the second we extract him he will bleed out and die."

"I agree. His blood pressure will drop like a rock and we'll lose him," Doc Freming said as he readied his largest-bore IV needle. While it's unusual for a flight surgeon to admit that a situation is beyond his training, it was even more shocking to Al that Doc Freming turned to him for answers.

While flight surgeons are well trained in all aspects of definitive human care, most do not specialize in emergency medicine, at least I have not met one who does. During SAR cases they often lapse into full treatment mode and attempt to provide hospital-level care in an environment that screams Load and Go. It takes astute recognition and nerve to realize that treating patients in a clinical environment is not the same as on the stern of a shrimp boat in the middle of the Gulf. Doc Freming, to his credit, was smart enough to rely on the expertise of his assistant, rather than assume control.

"How do you want to handle this, Al?"

Yates had had plenty of time to contemplate what he wanted to do while help was arriving and had already formulated a plan. "Let's look for and plug major bleeders, start multiple large-bore IVs and prepare the MAST pants. Keep plenty of O2 flowing and transport as soon as he's cut loose."

"Sounds good to me. I'm not used to dealing with messes like this," Doc said.

Freming attached two 16-gauge needles to each of Rennee's arms, then opened the flow to maximum on the bags of Lactate Ringers, IV fluid often used to counteract shock and administer medications. The DC's cutting torch popped and hissed to life with the sharp blade of blue flame reduced to a fine point. Al opened the MAST pants and laid them on the deck next to the drum.

"Ok, let's get started," Al said as the blue flame bit into the cable. Al removed a glove and placed a bare hand on the rusty grimy cable close to Rennee's leg. The DC was cutting the cable as far from Rennee's leg as possible without getting too close to his face. Beads of sweat popped out on his goggled face as he worked. Slowly the strands of cable began to part. Al was feeling for signs of excessive heat, though he did not know what he would do if the cable became too hot—douse it with water maybe, but that might increase the chances of infection later. No matter, if they didn't get Rennee out there would be no later for him.

"We're running low on O2," Al said over the combined symphony of hovering helicopter, cutting torch, diesel engine, and sea noise. He left his post to have the captain pull the *Kentucky Daughter* close to the *C Voyager* to retrieve the additional oxygen bottles. The third helicopter of the day had delivered them moments before and was now making lazy circles, waiting.

Yates returned to the drum and found the DC concentrating on a second bite of cable. Doc Freming watched both the patient and the cable. Al's radio demanded his attention.

"How's it going, Al?"

"We're coming along, but it will be a little longer."

With the additional fluids being pumped into Rennee and the pressure of the cable being slowly released, the coppery smell of blood told of new bleeding. This was what Al feared, Rennee's life oozing from his wounds and washing out to sea.

"OK, let's everybody make sure we're ready to cut him loose. Doc, do you think you can start more IVs once Rennee is free?" Without waiting for an answer he continued talking his plan through, looking for holes and hoping for input from the other two men. "Once that final cable is cut free, even if the doc can start another IV, it will be important to get the MAST pants on as quickly as possible." They all nodded in acknowledgement as the DC returned his attention to the cable.

Al had been so distracted by the extraction he had momentarily forgotten about the litter and the impending hoists. No way would they be able to pass Rennee from one boat to another while strapped in a litter. Reflexively, Al reached for his radio. "I need the litter ASAP, plus I think we we'll have to hoist from this boat. I don't think we can get him across from one to another."

"Roger that. We'll hoist the litter to the *C Voyager*. Once you have the patient in it and ready to go we'll pick him up from the *Kentucky Daughter*. If that works out we'll get everybody off the same way. Just make sure the deck is clear of flying debris. The last thing we need is more victims." Al double clicked the mike of his radio, giving the signal that the message was received and understood.

Yates ran forward along the skinny walkway to the pilothouse. "Captain, a helo will be dropping a litter to the *C Voyager* any second now. As soon as it arrives let me know and move in for a pickup. After we get Rennee ready we'll be hoisting from the rear of your boat. The helicopter crew will come onto the radio to let you know what direction to steer. Any questions?" The captain nodded understanding

"Al…Al…" Doc Freming was yelling from the rear of the boat. Al ran back to the drum where the DC was slicing through the last few strands of cable.

"What's the plan once he's free?" Doc asked.

"Shit, I guess we'll have to slide him this way." Al waved his hand and arm toward the trio. It was the only possible way despite Rennee's trapped leg. The leg pinned between his shoulder blades and the deck was already ripped from the ball socket, and Al worried they might cause more damage when they dragged Rennee out. He quickly recovered from the wince of sympathetic pain his mind imagined and pointed to Rennee's left shoulder while he knelt to Rennee's right, indicating the doc should grab the other side. Doc Freming immediately understood and grasped Rennee under the arm. Both had to lean hard into the drum to reach the trapped man.

"Once that last cable is cut, I want you to roll his leg and the drum over as we free him," Al said to the DC, who nodded understanding while continuing to cut.

"All right, Doc, here we go," Al said as much to himself as to Freming.

"Let's be careful and not rip the IVs from his arm as we do this," Doc said.

The IV bags had been taped to the outward sides of the drum, the slim plastic tubes snaking their way down to Rennee's arms.

"OK, guys, that's it, he's free." The DC flipped the lever of the torch, killing the flame. He knelt and set the device on the deck then stood and grabbed Rennee's leg. "Ready."

"On three," Al instructed. "One…two…three." They pulled and heaved, dragging Rennee from under the massive round monster with the long steel cable for a tongue. Al supported the pinned foot as he slid along the slime-covered deck, though it did little good. Rennee's lifeless body lolled limply like a rag doll. The drum spun under the guiding paw of the DC as the body was removed. Rennee's other leg, little more than pulverized meat and bone, made a wet splat as it landed on the deck; the DC had guided it as far as possible before letting go.

Blood seemed to ooze from everywhere. Al's gloved hands slipped as he tried to maneuver Rennee next to the flat MAST pants lying on the deck. "All right Doc, we have to move his leg back into position to get these pants on him. You lift his hips and I'll move his leg." Doc Freming straddled Rennee to grasp and lift his pelvic bone as Al quickly spun Rennee's leg out from underneath him.

As EMTs we are trained to avoid moving deformed extremities if at all possible. During initial training we were told a story about a well-meaning highway patrolman who responded to an automobile accident and found a woman with a broken ankle that is pointed in an unnatural direction. He attempted to set it straight by moving it back upright and inline with her leg only to later learned that he had merely finished the 360 degree twist of her ankle. In Al's case he knew the risk and accepted it as impossible to avoid.

Al set the leg on the deck, hardly recognizing the mangled mess next to it as another human appendage. "Doc, if you will lift again, I'll slide the MAST pants under his waist."

With blood creeping everywhere and Al hesitated for a second, then said, "Now." Doc Freming lifted the shattered body and Al, on hands and knees, easily slipped the largest portion of the pants under Rennee's hips. Al jumped to his feet and with the doc's help set Rennee's legs on the two pants legs. He wrapped the nylon material over each leg attaching the Velcro closures, three on each leg and two on the mid-section. The stomach portion of the pants reached up to the bottom of the rib cage.

Earlier, Al had attached the rubber tubing to the bottom of each pant leg and the attachment point on the abdominal section. The rubber tubing ran down to a small rubber foot pump with individual closure valves. Al opened both leg valves and stepped on the pump until he heard the Velcro straps begin to part, indicating that the proper pressure had been reached. He did not stop to take Rennee's blood pressure, which would have been normal procedure. Instead he filled the abdominal section, knowing they needed to bring up Rennee's blood pressure quickly or he wasn't going to make it, and the squeezing of the MAST pants would apply pressure and help control the bleeding.

Doc was probing Rennee's arms for another vein when the captain called from the cockpit, "Hey. They're ready with the litter." Al was so engrossed with the problem at hand he hadn't heard the helicopter move in and hoist the litter to the *C Voyager.*

"Doc, if you can get another IV, great. If not, then just get a blood pressure, we need to move." Time was critical now that Rennee was free from the drum.

The burly DC followed Al forward as the captain of the *Kentucky Daughter* inched toward to the *C Voyager.* Again the ships drew closer, water sluicing between the hulls, as the rescuers reached across and grasped the hard metal of the litter. The crewman from the *C Voyager* had wrestled the awkward device from its landing spot to the forward port rail, the trail line used to deliver the litter became tangled in its lifting cables. As Al heaved the litter across the small patch of sea he snatched the trail line and began a fast hand-over-hand retrieval. He knew they would need it for the hoist to come.

"Thanks, dude," Al said, not knowing the man's name. He and the DC hustled aft, Al reaching for his radio with his free hand.

"Seven six, swimmer," he called as they set the litter on the deck beside Rennee. Engulfed in two different tasked, Al was mentally working through several obstacles as he did so. They needed to secure Rennee in the litter and safely hoist him into a helicopter, but Al knew that the lack of room and power would limit the number of men retrieved.

"Two nine, we will be ready for a patient pickup by the time you pull into a hover."

"Roger that, Al," Hudson's response came. "We'll be there in two." Hudson began descending the helicopter toward the *Kentucky Daughter,* as Al tucked the radio away and turned toward the doc and the DC. "Let's get him in the litter."

Al knelt and slid his forearms under the back of Rennee's head, said, "On my count I want you guys to roll him to the left onto his damaged leg. We roll up as a unit, slide the litter under, then roll him into the litter, all on my command."

"You," Al said, pointing at the other shrimpboat crewman. "Once we have Rennee on his side I want you to tilt the litter on its side, so there's no lip to get up over." The crewman nodded and knelt next to the crew of three Coasties, litter at the ready.

"One…two…three." They rolled the unconscious Rennee onto

his most injured limb to his left. "Ready down," Al said and they rolled Rennee flat.

The screeching of the helicopter was unbearably loud now as Al again reached for his radio. "Seven six, swimmer."

"Go ahead, Al."

"Roger that, sir. We might want to hoist the doc first. He'll need to monitor the IVs he started, something I'm not allowed to do. Once the litter is in the helo, we won't have the room to pick him up." There was a slight delay as the helicopter crew thought this problem over, Then Hudson replied, "Tell the doc to be ready to go."

Al glanced skyward before returning his attention to the litter straps. Thick black nylon webbing with long stretches of Velcro, they had to be attached in the right order and in the correct location to ensure that a patient didn't accidentally make an early exit. Within seconds Al was lifting the litter's steel hoist cables to keep them clear of the webbing straps. Still on his knees he turned toward the open door of the helicopter, now hovering 50 feet high and 20 feet to starboard, and gave a thumb up. He was ready for pick up.

"All right, I'll cover the patient with my body to keep debris off him. Doc let the basket hit the deck to discharge the static electricity, then jump in. I'll send the patient up after you're in the helo." Nods all around.

Al knelt to shield Rennee's upper torso and face with his body and Rennee's face with his hands, taking care not to block the man's airway. In the aircraft Bill Munn slid the thumb wheel on the hoist control causing the rescue basket to glide smoothly down. With ten seconds of conning commands and careful, practiced cable management, the basket lightly bounced to a stop ten feet aft of the crowd on the *Kentucky Daughter's* deck.

This was the first hoist directly to the *Kentucky Daughter*, instead of the *C Voyager*. Bits of seaweed, crusted salt and dried ocean mud swirled and bit the faces of those huddled under the hurricane-force winds. Doc half rose and in a crouched run scuttled to the basket, plopping in the bottom of it. Almost as soon as the doc's butt hit the hard metal frame it was whisked skyward, so smoothly that Doc did not realize he had left the relative safety of the shrimper until, he felt the roaring air wind around him.

Doc Freming was sucked into the gaping mouth of the helicopter, disappearing into the dark hole. Inside the small airframe Bill pointed to the side of the basket, and the doc immediately understood, he was to jump from the basket, keeping low to avoid hitting his head on either the overhead or the arms of the rescue basket. Bill released the hoist hook and guided it to a holding pattern outside the cabin door, while he folded the arms of the basket and stuffed it into the tight storage compartment. If he had hoisted the patient first they would never have been able to hoist the doc too.

With the doc safely stored to one side and the patient already in a litter on deck it was a simple matter of sending down the bare hook and retrieving their prize. Bill returned his attention to the open door and said, "Part two complete, ready for litter pickup of patient."

Still hovering inches above his patient, Al stole another glance skyward and with relief saw the hoist hook descending through the humid air. The hook hit the deck and danced in small measured circles just a few feet from Al and his patient. Al leaned over, exposing Rennee to the rotor wash, as he snatched the hook up and secured the litter lifting cables. The weak link end of the trail line that he had earlier stuffed under his EMT equipment was snapped to the small non-lifting eye of the hoist hook. The taped bags of IV solution were ripped from the drum; Al forced them onto the hoist hook where they jiggled slightly in the helicopter's downward blasts of air. He bent back at the waist to spy the aircraft above and signaled for a pickup.

The cable slack magically disappeared as Bill rolled the thumb wheel upward until the taut cable eased Rennee from the deck of the *Kentucky Daughter.*

Al guided the trail line through his hands, to be sure the litter did not spin under the powerful influence of the helicopter's rotor blades. Seconds later Rennee disappeared into the helicopter as well. The trail line fluttered out the open door and sailed free toward the deck, because with Rennee inside the trail line could be discarded. Al piled the loose polypropylene line aside and keyed the mike of his radio.

The colossal stress of having a patient so badly mangled and so near death lifted from Al's shoulders, and once again he could feel the sweat stinging his eyes and the roll of the gulf under his feet. "Just a warm summer day, people enjoying the beach," he thought as he called for a pickup.

Rennee was long gone from Al's care by the time the helicopter landed back at the air station. His shoulders slumped from the heat, his body soaked with sweat, and his short hair plastered to his head, he was looking forward to hoping into a cool shower when heard his name over the loudspeaker near at the aircraft ramp: "Now Petty Officer Yates, report to Operations." Al dropped his gear in the shade of the open hangar door to enter the station's air-conditioned nerve center. It seemed that every person not assigned to this mission, as well as all of the participants, were huddled in the cramped office. All eyes turned to Al, and someone asked, "How was it?"

Al sucked in a muted breath in the deathly silence, "This guy was really fucked up..."

For months afterward, every time Al heard the SAR alarm he thought of this case. In the course of his career he faced numerous other tests, including a rare instance where he had to disentangle a military pilot from his chute after an ejection, but none required more from him or gave him as much in return.

Though Rennee lost a leg and the ability to walk, he lived through that horrible day and is still alive as I write this, just one among many who survived through Al's lifetime of heroic rescue efforts.

CHAPTER 10

Dire Straits

Not long after Castro's navy fired on the fleeing freighter, thousands more Cubans put to sea in every conceivable type of craft, from inner tubes tied together to full-fledged boats. Many died at sea, spent days or weeks without food or water, or lost family members to sharks. For the entire summer of 1994 the aircrews from Clearwater and Miami and numerous cutters scoured the ocean between the Keys and Cuba trying to save them all.

I had been in Key West for two weeks, flying every day and rescuing countless rafters, when I met the refugee I remember best. It was late afternoon and the sun was setting, our cabin half full of survivors, when we found another raft with five men. This was my ninth deployment, all free falls, into the bottomless blue water of the Florida Straits. I would have been sweating in my shorty wetsuit that day except that I was still wet, which kept me cool between deployments. Sliding to the open aircraft door I waited on the tap on my chest telling me to release my gunner's belt. The sun was splashing vivid color across the clouds as it dropped to the horizon. "Feeding time," I thought.

I swam to the raft as if I were jogging only to learn that the survivors and I had no common language. I had yet to meet a rafter who spoke English, and I spoke no Spanish. With a hovering helicopter, a rescue basket dangling below it, and a rescue swimmer at the edge of their raft, they knew what we wanted. I pointed at one man and waved for him to jump in the water with me, hoping to encourage them to enter the water one at a time instead of all five at once. The first four men patiently waited their turn as one by one I swam them away from the raft and hoisted them from the water. It was the fifth and last man who surprised me.

As I glided through the water, propelled by my fins, and waved for this last survivor to jump, he shook his head and crossed his arms. I waved my hand a little more emphatically and looked at the raft, wondering if I could puncture it with my knife and wait for him to join me. I could stab the inner tubes, but the wood lashed to the top, would likely keep him afloat, so I discarded that idea. He responded to my encouragement by holding his hand vertical, placing it atop his head, and pointing at the water. I figured he was telling me there were sharks in the water, and he had spotted some of my toothy friends.

I shrugged and swam toward the raft as if about to join him, the notion had crossed my mind, if it was a choice between that and becoming part of the food chain. I made the OK signal with my right hand, as if I was agreeing with him, then stuck out my hand to shake on it and seal the deal between us. He smiled and reached down to take my hand, thinking I had come to my senses. I clamped down on his hand and leaned back, yanking him from the raft, and almost lost my breath laughing as I went under.

But it was only funny to me for a second, because panic gripped the man and he wrapped his arms around my head in a bear hug, then climbed straight up, as if standing on my head would keep him out of the water. We went deeper. My training kicked in automatically and I used three powerful downward strokes. With my survivor clinging to my neck, I executed a front headhold release, spun him around, and placed him in a cross-chest control hold, then kicked for the surface.

Once we were again breathing air, I cinched down on his chest and finned away from the raft. He was still gasping, hyperventilating, as I moved toward the basket. No matter how hard I swam, we never moved away from the makeshift boat. I thought I was in a current that was moving us toward it, so I swam harder. Still, when I looked back it was ten yards behind us. The helicopter could not hover over a raft like this without endangering the aircraft. The rotor wash was powerful enough to lift and toss it about.

I ducked underwater and felt like a knuckle head when I saw the yellow nylon rope this last survivor had tied around his waist and to the raft. I reached under him, pulled my knife free from its pocket on my harness, and sawed the rope in two. It felt like a slingshot release as I swam free and put some distance between the raft and us.

With eyes the size of silver dollars and his face frozen in terror, my survivor was plucked from the sea to safety. I turned around in the now-dark ocean, rolling in small 5-foot waves and thought, "I must be seventy miles offshore, it doesn't get any better than this."

Eight years after my initial rescue swimmer training, this was the first time I had needed to use the lifesaving maneuver known as a release. The entire episode was comical instead of tragic because of my training, for which I was grateful. It also impressed upon me the need for real-world recurrent training.

Another SAR case that I think of as the Best Duty Day Ever also occurred in the Florida Straits. It was a Saturday in early spring 1997, and I was still assigned to Clearwater. I rarely looked forward to Saturday duty, especially on the Gulf Coast where we were most likely to respond to a false flare sighting rather than a real SAR case. It could mean a ruined weekend, but even that wasn't so bad. I loved my job, even on Saturdays.

Duty relief took place at 0800 hours sharp, and I had arrived early enough to check my gear and be ready to go well in advance. As we mustered the duty section for a head count and work assignments the SAR alarm blared to life: "Put the ready HH-60J on the line, missing diver off Key West."

The duty standers sprang to life to pull the helicopter from the hangar and we grabbed our gear and loaded it. We were in the air with almost 6000 pounds of fuel within fifteen minutes.

The pilot, Lt. Jim O'Keefe, a tall Irishman who likes to describe himself as better-looking than Tom Selleck, briefed the flight mechanic and me on the case as we flew south toward the Keys.

"We've got a diver missing from a dive boat since yesterday afternoon. Coast Guard Group Key West has a cutter and small boat searching, and the dive boat captain is also on scene looking."

They plugged the assigned search pattern into the computer as the flight mechanic and I readied the gear. I changed into my shorty wet suit and double-checked my EMT equipment. We learned from the Operations Center in Miami that the diver was experienced, had been on multiple dives the previous day, and was missing after the group's last dive. His wetsuit and spear gun should mean a greatly increased survival time. I had high hopes that we would find him.

After a two-hour transit flight we began our search between Key West and the Dry Tortugas. On the first leg, just minutes into what could turn out to be a long day of flying, I spotted someone out the left side in the water, frantically waving his arms. I interrupted the ongoing conversation immediately.

"I have a man in the water approximately half mile out at our eight o'clock," I said, meaning in relation to the nose of the aircraft. "Commence left turn."

O'Keefe banked a hard left as I kept a visual lock on the target and called out clock positions.

Eventually he said, "Have him in sight, commencing approach."

I scrambled from my seat and donned the rest of my gear before scooting hurriedly to the cabin door. The warm humid air washed over me as the flight mechanic opened the door, and the beat of rotor blades pounded my eardrums. We followed our normal procedures for a rescue swimmer free fall, and within 30 seconds of pulling into a hover I was swimming in calm tropical waters. The basket hoist of the survivor, followed by a harness pickup of myself, was all over in less than two minutes.

I yelled over the noise, "How long have you been in the water?"

"Eighteen hours."

He was still wearing his wetsuit and holding his spear gun when I picked him up. His only injuries seemed to be dehydration and exhaustion. I recommended that we take him to the hospital in Key West, and the pilots agreed. Our survivor was all smiles so excited he leaped across the floor of the helicopter to hug my neck.

"Can you put me down on that dive boat, so I can beat that captain's ass?" he was still grinning.

Once I had him rolled into the emergency room and gave a quick brief to the charge nurse, I handed him a special patch we had made up to give to survivors. Across the bottom it read, *I Have Been Rescued by the Very Best*, with a picture of a swimmer coming straight out of the patch toward the viewer. He was still talking excitedly when we shook hands and I left.

Thinking my day had started out pretty good, I relaxed during our flight back toward Clearwater. When we got close to Fort Myers the pilots elected to conduct a safety patrol along the beach, we were looking at bikinis. It was lucky that we did because a few miles north of town a 21-foot speedboat slammed into a smaller one broadside about 100 yards off the beach. The people in both boats spilled out as the crowd froze in shock.

Our co-pilot said, as he banked the helicopter around sharply, "Holy crap, did you guys just see that?" I had indeed seen it and immediately requested a sling deployment to hoist the injured.

In the water I had two uninjured survivors trying to climb back into their boat, several more survivors being pulled toward the beach by bystanders, and one unconscious man on the back of the smaller boat. I swam over and hurled myself onto the deck. There was another man on the boat, whether a passenger or a bystander from the beach I didn't know.

"Are you OK?" I asked him as I leaned over the unconscious man checking vital signs. I was multitasking, listening to one man while looking at the other.

He stated he was all right, so I enlisted his help with the hoist. We needed to transport the injured man immediately, as I could find no obvious signs of injury, yet he was unconscious. I surmised he might have sustained severe internal head trauma. With my bystander's help we hoisted our patient then myself and raced toward the local hospital just minutes away. After we flew back to the scene and found local EMS on the beach treating the rest of those involved, we turned back north for home.

The HH-60J burns an average of 1000 pounds of fuel per hour, more when fully loaded and gradually less as we lighten our weight. When we landed back at Clearwater at 2 PM we had been flying for exactly 6 hours, the maximum endurance of the helicopter. It is also the maximum number of allowable flight hours for a crew during a 24 hour day. We had saved two lives, flown as many hours as regulations allowed and not one minute more, and were granted liberty as the backup crew took over.

"This was even better than swimming seventy miles offshore at sunset," I thought as I walked to my car with the rest of my Saturday free.

I was comfortable as a swimmer but had some initial trepidation about my new job. When I arrived at Clearwater from Mobile I was assigned as the rescue swimmer shop supervisor. This was the Coast Guard's largest rescue swimmer shop, and I had 26 rescue swimmers working for me. I was responsible for being personally prepared, as well as making sure those in my charge did not fail either. This new dimension added more weight to my psychological load. I had not yet conquered my fear.

CHAPTER 11

Something Missing

My skills as a rescue swimmer had greatly improved from years of experience. But something was still missing.

The list of responsibilities of a shop supervisor was enormous and included but was not limited to the tracking and maintenance all life-support equipment, maintaining the duty schedule, ensuring physical fitness standards were met and flight minimums maintained, making certain EMT recurrent skills stayed sharp, and solving all problems. I floundered under the stress. I had inherited 26 Type A, jock-molded rescue swimmers. If I failed, more than just my life or the lives of my survivors hung in the balance. I knew I still had much to learn. For the first time since my stint in New Orleans I was without a mentor.

That is not to say I did not have a boss or a clear chain of command, because I did. But having a chain of command does not necessarily mean I had a mentor, someone whose example I could follow, who could teach me what I still did not know. By this time too I had been a swimmer long enough and from the early stages of the program that I was about as experienced a rescue swimmer as anyone the Coast Guard could assign. The weight on my shoulders became more burdensome with my added responsibilities, until Senior Chief George Waters became my new supervisor.

Waters was not your typical rescue swimmer. He was an Aviation Survivalman (ASM) before the Coast Guard had made it mandatory for all ASMs become rescue swimmers. Before any of them became swimmers, ASMs maintained survival equipment and flew in other aircrew positions. Waters was one of the few who transitioned over and obtained the collateral qualification of rescue swimmer. My path to becoming a swimmer had been hard—Waters's path had been harder.

Waters was one of my instructors at my initial training in Elizabeth City, but when I was there he had not yet attempted the school in Pensacola. Elizabeth City was the perfect place to train, and Waters took advantage of his time there. He was aware that the Coast Guard had made the collateral qualification mandatory for all ASMs who were E-6 and below, and he knew equally well that Farmer would enforce this mandate.

His first attempt to pass the school landed him in the hospital with pneumonia, such a bad case that the doctors removed a portion of one of his lungs. Waters thought this might be the end of his career and that he certainly had no chance to pass the school. Yet with a determination that defies reason he spent months conditioning himself and, once he received medical clearance, headed back to Pensacola.

This time he did not fail. He met the challenge, yet knew that his condition meant that Coast Guard doctors would never allow him to use the skills he had earned. He would always be limited to another aircrew position.

I far exceeded Waters in rescue-swimmer experience, and when he arrived I was unsure how he might help with my burden. Waters's area of expertise was in life, not that he was so much older than myself, but that he was a student of life, how to live it well, what made people tick, how to motivate, when to encourage, when to correct. He was a master at living.

As I became accustomed to my new job and with Waters's guidance I began to enlarge my view of what it meant to be a rescue swimmer and what it meant to be in charge of rescue swimmers.

He gave me the freedom to pursue whatever I thought might aid us in success and keep failure at bay. We had open-water swims at the beach, joint training exercises with local fire-department personnel and dive-rescue teams, guest medical speakers, swim competitions, and many other activities that kept our skills sharp. I measured our success by the other swimmers' reactions at the end of a workday. If, once I granted liberty, the guys lingered in the shop, made small talk, and seemed satisfied, then I considered the activities successful. And if we saved lives without loss or injury to ourselves I considered us successful. By my measurements we were very successful—as rotary winged rescue swimmers.

This was my first unit that had both helicopters and fixed-wing aircraft, in this case C-130-HC Hercules. Often the most recognizable aircraft in the world, this plane has been in production since the 1950s. It has four large engines, the airframe houses a massive cargo bay, and is piloted from an elevated flight deck. One of the main reasons for its popularity is that the aircraft can be modified for many different missions.

At Air Station Clearwater we outfitted nine C-130s with an enormous amount of survival equipment and rescue gear. And, as unlikely as it seemed, we had six rescue swimmers flying in them—not as swimmers—but as drop masters, load masters, or basic aircrewmen. Before my posting to this unit I had very little contact with the personnel who flew these big planes. As a new shop supervisor I learned about the aircraft and its mission. Additionally, I had to assign men to fly in them, forcing them to turn their backs on their swimmer skills, skills so incredibly difficult to earn that they are not easily set aside.

I listened to my guys after they returned from myriad missions and detected the foul stench of failure in the stories they recounted. If they found survivors during a search, they would call in another unit to complete the rescue—if possible. If not, then those in distress were not rescued. When they located a medical patient they could do little more than offer encouragement. They could drop a pump to a sinking boat. Among all the things they could do, they still could not provide definitive rescue. The look on my guys faces reminded me of the rescue dogs sent to search for survivors in the aftermath of a disaster. The dogs' owners occasionally hid themselves in the rubble or mud so the dog could find a live person, keeping the dog's spirits up. It made them search harder and provided joy in the midst of misery. My SAR "dogs" had no such relief.

During one of my candid conversation with Waters he encouraged me to pursue a solution and offer it up the chain of command. I pondered this for many months and finally decided I would research and propose that rescue swimmers be deployed, via parachute, from the back of C-130s. From January 1998 to July of that same year I snatched every free moment I could and read old SAR case folders, researched pararescue schools, detailed where, how, and why we should be providing this service. I also believed the files from just one unit were not enough to provide a balance picture. I called ASM2 Shawn Whaley in Sacramento, another Coast Guard C-130 unit, and asked him to compile the same information and forward it to me. I believed strongly that this was an ability we needed, but under Waters's urging decided to let the research speak to the need. Wisely he explained that letting others draw the same conclusion from the information I had was more powerful than telling them it was so.

I am often shocked at the discrepancies between what the public perceives are our capabilities and what we are actually allowed to do. Many outsiders I spoke to during my career could not believe we did not provide SCUBA rescue, that we were not paramedics, and that we could not jump out of aircraft with parachutes. This disconnect between what we could do and what others thought we could do meant no one was pushing for a service that they thought we already provided.

Our research showed that during fiscal year 1996, between both units, the Coast Guard would have likely requested a pararescue team be on the aircraft 64 times and would have likely deployed them 25 times. In Sacramento they did deploy Air Force PJs twice during 1996, the year we based our research on.

As I relayed this information to Waters he pointed out numerous mitigating factors. If we are already task saturated, how can we request additional tasking? How can we ensure the safety of our pararescue teams? Is there an alternative that is more cost effective? At first I thought he was trying to thwart my idea. But as I busily researched the answers to these questions I realized he was merely preparing my position paper for the inevitable roadblocks.

In August of 1998, after review by my command, my letter requesting the creation of pararescue capabilities was forwarded to Coast Guard Headquarters, where it promptly sank out of sight. I had hoped to learn that the idea might be studied, or that a unit might be created to conduct research and development. At the very least I had hoped to learn a decision could be made one way or the other. The submission of this letter was the final death of my young naiveté. My time on the Stan Team, where I had witnessed to great change, had led me to the false assumption that great change was possible, that decision-makers within the Coast Guard were capable of considering improvements, and that they actively sought ideas on how to improve from those assigned to complete the missions. Apparently I had failed to be convincing enough. I certainly believed I had failed my guys who were assigned to fly on those aircraft, and failed those we could have rescued had this idea been adopted. Even though I shared these failures with the Coast Guard, the weight of my part in it was crushing my spirit.

CHAPTER 12

Elizabeth City

By the time I was due to transfer out of Clearwater I had been on hundreds of rescues and lost count of how many lives I had saved. My next assignment took me back to Elizabeth City, North Carolina, the summer of 1999. By then I was supremely confident in my abilities as a rescue swimmer but still harbored my secret fear of failure. With this fear always lurking in the recesses of my mind I longed for the chance to exorcise my personal demon.

On 16 September 1999 I thought I might have my chance. A Category One hurricane named Floyd limped ashore, causing little damage to the shoreline or ships at sea. But Floyd's rain unleashed torrents of water that flooded the Tar River Basin and parts of inland North Carolina. I had duty the night Floyd made landfall, and initially all was quiet. We flew a safety over-flight of the channel leading into the Norfolk River to look for missing channel markers, without which ships might run aground. Later that night, though, the SAR alarm blared to life: "Put the ready HH-60J on the line, three hundred people stranded on rooftops in vicinity of Tar River."

"Did they say three hundred? Naw, they had to mean three," I thought.

I ran from the swimmer shop on the far side of the parking lot from the hangar, toward the ramp, where the line crew was already pulling the helicopter out. When I saw Lcdr Jim Watson running from the Operation Center I knew it had to be serious. Watson was known for his unflappable calm.

"Let's go, I'll brief in the air," he said as we all headed for the waiting aircraft.

We were airborne within minutes, and Watson told us there were reports of hundreds of stranded people on their roofs and that the Tar River had risen to 45 feet above flood stage. There were no divert facilities to get fuel, nor was he sure where we were going to take the survivors.

Normally streetlights, businesses, homes, and countless other light sources would have illuminated the ground below us like stars. On that night all was an inky blackness, and Watson had to rely on night vision goggles (NVGs) to avoid power lines, towers, trees, and other obstacles.

Flashlights began piercing the night sky as the noise of our helicopter alerted survivors to our passing. Watson set the bird down in the middle of Interstate 65, at a makeshift landing zone set up by the North Carolina State Police. We picked up a trooper and lifted off again to search for the specific house where the residents were in immediate danger of drowning. In the absence of a known latitude and longitude position, we hoped the trooper could identify landmarks and lead us to the people that had made the call. We followed his directions, bypassing urgent lights signaling us as we flew by.

"There are a lot of flashlights out there, sir," I told Watson. I was thinking we were passing by many in need to rescue others and wasn't sure we were pursuing the best course of action. Under the guidance of the Trooper we found the correct neighborhood, but could not identify the specific address from which the call had come My personal dark fear edged toward the surface and I was about to voice my concerns when, before I spoke up, Watson had come to the same conclusion.

"Let's get in there," he said as he surveyed the damage through his NVGs.

The rain had let up to a minimal drizzle and the winds had died down from its original hurricane strength, but we were still bouncing around. Watson pulled into a hover over a pallet-manufacturing company in response to multiple lights being waved in our direction.

"Jerry, are you ready?" he said and, of course I was.

As I was lowered between the power lines, trees, parked trucks, and stacks of pallets I was thankful for Watson's ability to hold a hover in such tight confines. I began to spin as I approached the loading dock where we had seen the lights and started counting before my feet even hit the raised cement pad. Ten faces turned to cover their eyes from the blast of the rotor wash, then the pallets starting flying. I held my hands out to fend them off, batting and kicking them as they were lifted by the helicopter's wind. As soon as I touched down I released the hook and waved the aircraft back.

Inside the warehouse there were two crying kids, several adults looking at me expectantly, and the pickup truck they had driven up the ramp.

"We saw the water rising and started to drive out of town, but the water kept getting deeper. We're not all related," the man said, waving his hand around, indicating the others, "we just picked up people as we drove. We made it as far as this warehouse."

He also told me the water was rising at about six inches per hour and by his estimation had not slowed for the last couple of hours, even though the rain was letting up. I believed the Tar River provided the major drainage for this low-lying part of the state and agreed the water would continue to rise for some time.

"OK, let's keep kids and families together." I knelt down in front of the smallest child, a boy of about three. "Are you ready to go?"

I told him I could send him and his older brother, a boy of about thirteen up together, and asked him if that was all right. He nodded and buried his head in his brother's pants leg. Their mom nodded, and I told her she would follow.

Watson agreed we should hoist two at a time if they could fit, and within seconds the flight mechanic had the basket on the way down.

I pulled the tethered basket under the protective overhang where flying debris wouldn't hit us and showed the boys where to sit.

"If you're brave I'll give you my patch," I told the youngest and pointed at the rescue swimmer patch on my shoulder. He nodded as I gave the thumbs up and the basket ascended.

Watson held a hover in the tight quarters for all eight hoists and ten survivors. When it was my turn, I had to abandon the safety of the building and prepare to do battle once again with the pallets and debris. As I rose through the storage yard, the pallets took to the air just as I had expected. To avoid them Watson and the flight mechanic worked together and attempted to keep me clear, but as the aircraft lurched sideways I saw the building approach faster than I was being raised. I kicked my feet around and, with not even a second to spare, fended myself off the wall. I spun out of control and contacted the roof with my back. A second later I was clear of the building and swinging wildly, as Watson had compensated for my inadvertent contact by moving back toward the yard. By then, though, I was clear of all the flying debris and on my way up. I did a quick check of all my body parts before I reached the door of the helicopter, to see palpable relief on the mechanic's face.

I crawled across the deck and looked at the cramped faces seeking out the littlest one, then I ripped my patch away from the Velcro holding it and stuck it to his shirt.

While I was out of the aircraft Watson had been assessing the number of survivors, not just the ones we were hoisting, but all those represented by all the lights we had seen. The co-pilot had been busy talking to the State Police, identifying a landing zone and triage point. By the time I had returned and listened in on the ICS, Watson had already formulated a plan, and we made top speed to the improvised drop zone.

Back at home plate, Watson's dire request for every available asset had created a wave of phone calls. Aircrews were hustling in, aircraft were being fueled.

The co-pilot had radioed ahead, so the troopers were ready for us when we landed. I hopped out of the aircraft once we were on deck and spoke with the first officer I reached. He would direct the survivors, and they would continue to set up for as many as we could bring. I escorted my survivors and the officer we had originally picked up from the helicopter and jumped back in.

"Let's rock and roll," I said over the ICS.

The hunt was on, and it didn't take us long to find more survivors in need of rescue. Watson decided to head for the river, believing that those trapped closest would be in the gravest danger. On this sortie we never got all the way to the river, opting instead to drop down to a neighborhood of doublewide mobile homes. Flashlights hailed us from almost every house.

The pounding of rotor blades was deafening as I was smoothly delivered to the roof. I shimmied over to the edge and jumped to the deck below as wide-eyed survivors watched. A head count revealed thirteen souls; half were kids, and one was in a wheelchair.

"Time to get to work," I thought as I pulled my radio from my pocket to call Watson.

"We're running low on fuel," he said, "but we've got help on the way."

I explained to the gathered crowd in the trailer's living room, "OK, we're going to keep one kid with each adult and try and get as many as possible. But we won't be able to get you all. There are more helicopters on their way. Are we ready?"

We were on the third hoist when I heard Watson's familiar voice over the radio, "We're out of time, on the next hoist we're sending the bare hook for you." I responded to his call and explained to the remaining survivors that we would have to leave. As I was talking I heard the distinctly different sound of the twin rotor-head Chinook. A Marine helicopter had pulled into a hover behind my HH-60J and was waiting for us to vacate.

I gave a little wave as I was yanked skyward. We dropped the survivors at the makeshift landing zone out on the interstate. While we had been working it seemed to me that everybody in the state had been mobilized. There were aircraft landing on both sides of us, ambulances lined the underpass in front of us and police, firemen and EMS personnel were either directing people or providing treatment.

During our return to the air station in Elizabeth City, Watson explained that the command was contacting every DOD and civilian resource they could think of, because the extent of the flooding was much more widespread than originally reported and getting worse. Requests for assistance were flooding in from all around the Tar River Basin, and a long stretch of I-95 had been closed.

"Once we fuel up we're headed back out," Watson said. "Does everybody feel up to it?" By now my adrenaline was flooding into my system, and I felt like I could lift an entire house from its foundation. I think we all felt the same.

Throughout the rest of that night I was hoisted to roofs, windows and the loft of a barn. Using the aircraft's crash ax, I chopped my way into second-floor windows and flooded cars. I could hear my fellow swimmers over the radio doing the same. I lost count of how many people we picked up that night.

Eight hours after our initial call we landed back at the air station to pass our aircraft over to a fresh crew. I still felt strong and approached my executive officer, Cdr. Rod Ansley, as he walked purposefully across the tarmac to get a brief from Watson.

"Let me go back out there, sir. I still feel good."

He smiled. "I bet you do, but we've got a fresh crew waiting on your helo. Go home and get some rest. Be back in ten hours and you can go again."

As I looked around and noted the four helicopters surrounded by fueling and ground handling crews, I knew he was right.

I was back at work early the next morning, having slept a couple of hours. Shortly after my transfer to Elizabeth City, the current shop supervisor, AST1 Darren Reeves, was promoted and transferred out. The job had been placed squarely on my shoulders and by then I had grown comfortable with the responsibility.

Coast Guard, Army, Navy, and Marine aircraft were arriving from all points, and I hustled help from every corner. I visited the AST School, solicited help from the instructors, and even put some students to work fabricating trail lines. We cleaned and inspected gear that had been used the night before and I assigned swimmers to aircraft as they became available. I didn't get a chance to go out again until later that night.

By the second night the skies were full of aircraft. My CO and XO, Captain Odom and Cdr. Ansley, had arranged for an AWACS (the Navy's radar-equipped, fixed-wing P-3 Orion aircraft) to provide air traffic control and had set up a temporary triage center at a local high school and a forward command center and still had more Coast Guard aircraft on their way. They had gone with less sleep than I had in the last 24 hours.

The around-the-clock rescue efforts went on for three days, and more than 2000 people were rescued by the combined forces my command had amassed. We had used the vertical-surface rescue technique extensively during that time and used a few tricks that had not previously existed. While mentally I noted what we had done, how we did it, and what we could do to improve, I kept my focus on swimmers, the center of my sphere of influence.

By the summer of 1999 I was experienced enough that I finally had something of value to share with my fellow swimmers. By accepting responsibility for those under my charge I was compounding my chance for failure by a factor of 12, the number of swimmers in my shop. Because this was a self-imposed mandate without a specific timeline, I thought I could plan for any eventuality. I decided my swimmer shop would be the best, most professional, most hard core, mentally tough swimmers in the Coast Guard.

But it wasn't until early the next year, when my new senior chief checked in, that I truly began to implement my program. Once again I was under the helpful guidance of George Waters and I made use of the enormous amount of trust and freedom he granted me to start my program.

The premise of my program was training. Having studied past aircraft crashes and being well versed on most of the major swimmer accidents since the beginning of the program, I knew that human beings typically react as we are trained to do. And because rescue swimmers almost always fly in alone, without a second swimmer, I knew I would not be there when my guys made tough decisions, faced the unexpected, or became physically exhausted. My only option was to train them for every eventuality I could think of.

First came the training of potential rescue swimmers. At the beginning of the program during the 1980s, there was no buildup before entering AST School. But in the mid 1990s the Coast Guard started its Airman Program. The idea was to take those who wanted to attend an aviation school from their present unit (often a small-boat station or cutter) and introduce them to aviation. These airmen learned the basic rudimentary skills, such as fueling, towing, danger zones, etc. For those who wanted to be rescue swimmers, it was a chance to build up to the physical standards required to get into the school. Four months prior to a candidates' class convening date they would be sent to the air station nearest their present unit for this program.

At Elizabeth City, in order to build leadership and introduce potential swimmers to the latest version of the school, I assigned a recently graduated rescue swimmer from my shop as a mentor. I monitored the progress of both the potential student and mentor. We created special exercises for anyone who exhibited weakness. As a shop we spent the first two hours each day working out, and during that workout we identified a student's weakness then created a special buildup for him or her.

One such idea was to have a student roll a single die, the type that typically hangs from a rearview mirror, note the number showing and multiply it by 100. That number represented how many pushups, pullups or situps the student had to do. They could do them in sets, but they had to complete them before the end of the workday. With the help of my guys we developed many such ideas and used them to create the most successful Airman Program in the Coast Guard. Any individual who completed our program had a 90 percent chance of passing the school, while other units typically had about a 50 percent return rate on their students.

I was extremely pleased with guys' response to being mentors and equally pleased with the success of my potential students. That was not to say we did not suffer setbacks. One such setback had me in Waters's office asking for more time. Claude Morrisse was an airman who I felt had potential to be a great swimmer. His mentor felt likewise, but Claude was such a large man, at 250 pounds, that he had difficulty completing the pullups. In fact, during his four months in the Airman Program, Claude could not do a single pullup. As his class date drew near I went to Waters and asked him to buy more time with headquarters and re-assign Claude to a later school.

While it was extremely unusual for such a request to be granted, Waters trusted my judgment and made the necessary phone calls. It was not an easy request for him to grant.

"Claude, how badly do you want to be a rescue swimmer?" I asked him.

He responded with what I had decided was a prerequisite that every swimmer must possess, but one that we could not give them. "The only way I will fail is if I die," he said. That was just what I wanted to hear, and I sat down at the sewing machine to fabricate what Claude would later call the Anti-Christ Belt.

I sewed a thick webbing belt that fastened around his waist, with two straps that hung alongside each leg. At the bottom of each strap was a snap hook and ring, on which we fastened a cinder block. Claude had to complete negatives on the pullup bar with this belt and the cement blocks. His mentor had to assist him to the bar and have his chin reach above it. He would then lower himself on a slow four count. Claude's daily total was based upon the fuzzy die he threw at the end of each workout. He did hundreds of negative pullups each day. Negatives are very effective at tearing down muscle, and a body's reaction to this is to rebuild the muscle stronger than it was. However, it is an extremely painful process. Despite the sheer physical pain it took, Claude eventually became able to complete eight pullups each time he mounted the bar, the minimum number required to pass the school. Claude went on to graduate from swimmer school and is now one of the best rescue swimmers in the Coast Guard.

Another aspect of my program concentrated on nonstandard rescues that my swimmers might face. I coordinated joint training exercises with Cole Yates, the manager of the Kitty Hawk lifeguards. He and his fellow lifeguards gave us classes and surf swims on riptides and breaking waves.

Our unit responded to several car accidents along the Outer Banks, and as a result I contacted the local fire department and coordinated an auto-accident extraction exercise. We also learned about the challenges of communicating with those departments that do not use marine-band radios.

As a direct result of lessons learned in the aftermath of Floyd, I spearheaded the building of a three-story training tower, with windows, to practice vertical surface rescues. My guys and I trained on this building at least once a year.

When Bill Curtis of the Secret Service contacted me about assisting with his on-going rescue swimmer program, I eagerly jumped at the chance to involve my guys. Bill trains Secret Service agents to be rescue swimmers in order to protect the president and the first family when they are on the water. We spent a couple of weeks each year facilitating their training and participating in the offshore swim exercises. I also introduced Bill to Cole Yates, thinking Yates could provide exactly the type of training Bill was looking for.

My swimmers eagerly dove into whatever training exercise I devised, and I devised many, from dewatering drills with intentionally sabotaged pumps, medical drills based upon actual cases, and miles and miles of open-water swims, just to name a few. Then I challenged them to devise their own training scenarios for the rest of us. I tried to turn everything into a competition. Waters had observed that swimmers who see something as a competition often respond like a NFL linebacker with a free shot at the quarterback. He was right again and my program flourished because of it.

I had embarked upon a five-year program that I hoped would ripple out, be refined, and re-used by those that had been there for it. In the process my guys and I had faced many challenges, personal and professional.

By the middle of 2001 *Coast Guard Magazine*, published by our headquarters, printed an article celebrating the 4000th life saved by rescue swimmers since the beginning of the program. Shortly after that article was released, another ship began to sink off the coast with 34 souls on board, the same number of as were on the *Marine Electric*. After the men on that later ship were saved by two rescue swimmers, Bob Florisi and Darren Reeves, I considered it poetic justice that those 34 men were saved by men whose jobs had been created by an eerily similar incident 18 years before.

One of my youngest swimmers, Dave Foreman, spent the night in the hospital after he went into oil-filled seas to rescue survivors of a tanker fire and sinking. His story is prominently featured in Martha's book, *So Others May Live*.

In my opinion, my swimmers were by far the best prepared group in the Coast Guard, and they proved it to me over and over.

This tour had transformed me from learner to teacher, a change I hoped would alleviate my fear of failure, even though that fear was often the driving force behind my tireless efforts.

A good friend and flight mechanic, Mike "Klink" Klinkefus, would often stand at the open hangar door with me, look up at the weather, and say, "Nope, not shitty enough for guys as experienced as us. Let's send a new guy." He had tapped into a new feeling I was experiencing. I wanted something that challenged me, tested my mettle as a man, and taught me something.

CHAPTER 13

A Long Good Night

Even in the earliest stages of my training program, proof that it was working and also that swimmers would rather die than fail came on Memorial Day, 29 May 2000. As was my custom I encouraged rescue swimmers to report what they did to those of us not involved, hoping to glean some lessons for all of us. This story is a melding of what all three swimmers shared in the days following that long night.

Rick Bartlett stands tall and lanky with creases pinching the corners of his eyes. A consummate professional and experienced pilot, he was the aircraft commander that Monday morning as he and the rest of the duty section relieved the offgoing crew at 8:00 AM sharp. Rick Bartlett was a lieutenant commander whose collateral duty, when not flying, was the rotary wing operations officer. He decided when, where, and how the helicopters assigned to the air station in Elizabeth City, North Carolina, would be used. While doing so he was to keep the operations officer and commanding officer informed and follow their directions.

When an aircraft commander reports for duty, he or she first checks the weather, as it is of pivotal importance. Bartlett strode with his usual air of purpose around the Operations Center where a junior officer manned the desk. A metallic console housed the myriad radios, phones, and related equipment. The windowed room overlooks another room with a large chart table and a wall-mounted TV that displays the weather round the clock for anywhere on the planet. Bartlett checked the marine forecast and was immediately drawn to the picture of a growing low-pressure system plowing through northeast North Carolina. Winds were to reach 30 knots with heavy rain, moderate turbulence, and dropping temperatures. He planned to monitor the situation closely.

Bartlett's swimmer for the 24 hour shift was Doug Hanley. Doug is the life of every party. Looking like an offensive lineman, I wondered how he moved with so much speed when we swam or ran. He is a family man with the requisite wife, kids, and dog, who loves to drink beer and hug, usually in that order, and it doesn't matter who gets wrapped up by his massive arms; everyone is a target.

A workaholic by nature, Doug spent the early part of the duty day wrapping expended trail lines for reuse, inspecting life rafts, and similar jobs. These tasks fill our everyday existence and are the lifeblood of our profession. His self-imposed workday lasted until just before 4:00 PM.

By late in the afternoon Bartlett realized the forecast had woefully underestimated the storm's intensity. Winds by then had exceeded 40 knots, and slanting, slamming raindrops pelted the closed hangar doors. Around 4:00 PM Bartlett was ordered by District Five Operations Center to rescue the crew of the sailing boat *Irish Mist*, a 36-foot transatlantic boat with two Australian crewmen and their dog on board. The reportedly anemic storm had turned vicious once it moved offshore, and the crew of the *Irish Mist* had suffered several violent knockdowns. A knockdown is the term used when a boat, usually a sailboat, is tossed onto its side so that the mast or superstructure contacts the water. Those on board were willing to abandon ship despite, or maybe because of, the 30-foot seas.

Bartlett punched the SAR alarm button and calmly voiced the mission over the public address system: "Now put the ready HH-60J on the line, sailing boat taking on water ninety miles offshore." He then picked up the phone and dialed the helicopter watch captain and ordered extra weight bags and trail lines thrown onto the aircraft. He also requested the aircraft be fueled to maximum capacity.

This rescue started no differently from the hundreds of others in which Doug had played a part. He hurriedly dressed in his dry suit and other swimmer gear before hustling to the helicopter.

Bartlett briefed the crew what to expect from the wind and waves once they arrived offshore. Lieutenant Junior Grade (Ltjg) Randy Meador was the co-pilot assigned the left seat to provide navigation and communication assistance. Meador was very new, having been at the air station for about 30 days. Being prior enlisted helped ease some of his apprehension, but little, other than experience can prepare one for those conditions, and words cannot adequately describe being there.

Chris Manes eased up beside Doug at the helicopter for the mission brief. Chris worked on the aircraft's avionics when not standing duty as a flight mechanic. Doug was pleased to have someone he had flown with in the past as his hoist operator. Chris is a stout man with a sharp wit.

"We've got ceilings of one hundred to two hundred feet," Bartlett said. "Visibility is down to about a half mile. The winds are a steady forty-five knots with higher gusts. We don't want to run into anything, so let's be careful. Call out obstacles, don't assume we see something. Randy I filed a Special VFR" He was referring to Visual Flight Rules, which allow us to take off in those conditions. "I want you to plot a course down the Pasquotank River. This should keep us from flying into something we can't see."

Within minutes of the initial alarm the crew was taxiing to the large painted H on the tarmac.

"Tower, this is Rescue six zero three one, ready for take off and river departure to the east," Meader transmitted.

"Rescue three one, clear for take off, good hunting," the air traffic controller responded.

Bartlett lifted the collective and the heavy aircraft rose from the ground. He tilted the nose over, causing the helicopter to shudder against the wind as it clawed forward towards the river. Meador manned the radios with flight controllers, the radar, and navigation computer. Doug keyed the radio mike from his computer console in the rear to set up a guard with the Coast Guard Communication Unit in Chesapeake, Virginia, known as CAMSLANT (Communication Area Master Station for the Atlantic). Doug did this automatically and with the understanding he was to call in the aircraft position every fifteen minutes. If he missed a call the CAMSLANT radioman made a concerted effort to reestablish contact. Two missed calls and the "cavalry", in the form of every available Coast Guard asset, would be alerted.

The crew crossed the Outer Banks of North Carolina before dark.

The winds increased to a steady 50 knots, and the helicopter jolted roughly along the charted course. The wave tops were being ripped from the water, brown silt was stirred to the surface. The conditions reminded Bartlett of the numerous hurricanes into which he had flown.

Helicopter SAR cases occurring farther than 50 miles offshore are required, by policy, to be escorted by a fixed-wing aircraft: in this case a four-engined C-130 Hercules was to fly cover for the HH-60J. (Cover is the term used to describe the duties of the escort airplane).

"One five zero four, this is six zero three one on point eight," Meader called to establish a communication link.

"Three one from the O-four, we have divert information on a more pressing case when you're ready to copy," the radioman on the C-130 responded.

"Roger, send your traffic."

"The sailing boat *Cariad* has suffered an explosive knockdown." (an explosive knockdown is described as a roll greater than 120 degrees). "The rigging was ripped from the mast and the main hatch was washed overboard. A female crewman was injured and is bleeding profusely. An immediate divert is requested by District Operations."

While the crew of the *Irish Mist* was in dire straits, the crew of the *Cariad,* was in even greater need. The C-130 radioman transmitted the position of the *Cariad* and Meader plotted it into the helicopter computer. Only 15 miles from the scene, Bartlett banked the helicopter on the appropriate intercept course to the new target.

"We have a new mission and we are only about five minutes from the scene. Doug, why don't you get dressed out, if you haven't already." Doug was prepared.

"Chris, complete rescue check list part one."

"Randy, try to raise the *Cariad* on the radio and find out as much as you can."

Each crew member had his duties clearly defined. The response was immediate.

The helicopter crew communicated through the C-130 with the *Cariad* crew and learned that a 200-pound stove had landed on the female crewmember. She was bleeding from her head and was semi-conscious. The boat had no power and was dragging its mainsail to slow its momentum. Although sail boats are designed to move forward even without the aid of sails, the *Cariad* had enough freeboard on for the wind and waves to push it through the water at about five knots.

The captain was reported as saying, "I'm afraid another knock-down like that last one will cause her to sink. We're ready to abandon ship."

Once within radio range, Meader had activated the radio direction finder and locked onto their transmission. This gave the aircraft commander a course he compared to the position passed by the C-130 radioman. Sometimes information that has gone through several sources before reaching the rescue aircraft is unintentionally incorrect or old, and pilots must constantly update data to ensure a prompt response. Even with all the information they had, the pilots had trouble finding the white hull of the *Cariad* in the frothy white wave tops and spray.

The captain reiterated, "We have three people on board and we are ready to go."

After the helicopter crew spotted the boat, Bartlett flew in a tight circle to evaluate the seas and contemplate the logistics of the rescue. He estimated the waves to be running about 20 feet when compared to the 46-foot hull of the *Cariad*. Each member of the crew provided valuable insight, and Bartlett made quick decisions based upon his own vast experience and input from his team.

"Look at the lines and rigging dragging behind the boat. Do you think you think you can grab them and pull yourself aboard?" Bartlett asked Doug despite the nagging underlying question of whether he could deploy a swimmer into those seas and recover him.

"No problem."

"Complete part two for a sling deployment of the swimmer just aft of the boat," he ordered.

"Roger," Chris said. Seconds later he stated, "Part two complete, ready aft for sling deployment of rescue swimmer."

Doug slid toward the open door, dangled his feet outside the airframe, and sensed Chris's hand on the webbing of his harness. The whooshing of wind and scream of helicopter machinery replaced the static of the ICS.

One solid tap on his chest and Doug removed the gunner's belt. He quickly followed the motion with a thumb up then lowered his mask and bit down on the snorkel, tasting the dry acid bitterness that signaled the rush of adrenaline. The harness lifted his heavy body from the deck, and he swung to his right. Chris was facing him, waiting for the second signal that indicated Doug was ready to continue. Doug gave it and was immediately lowered below the aircraft. The aircraft faced the steady wind, pushing the rotor wash aft. The swirling air and choppy seas normally accompanying a hovering helicopter were forced back. Doug squinted upwards one last time, his vision filled with the hover lights illuminating the storm-darkened skies. He turned his attention back to the boat as he approached the water, then abruptly splashed into the water and disconnected from the hoist hook. Without a backward glance he gave the "I'm all right" signal and without interrupting his swim stroke powered his way up one hill of water and slid down the face of the next.

Despite the aircraft's buffeted hover, Chris had done his job extremely well and deposited Doug within a few feet of the line trailing the boat. But the *Cariad* was moving too fast and escaped Doug's reach within seconds of his entering the water. He signaled for a pickup. They had learned the first lesson of the night.

Chris expertly dropped the hook, with an open sling attached into the water next to Doug, who snapped his harness to it and was yanked from the sea.

With Doug safely inside the airframe and hooked up to the ICS again, they discussed a new approach. Bartlett settled on a course of action and repeated it to ensure that everyone understood.

"We will deploy Doug on his harness and have all three survivors enter the water simultaneously. Doug will retrieve them one at a time until we have hoisted all three."

The plan was understood, and Meader spoke to the crew of the boat while Doug and Chris prepared to do another deployment.

Bartlett was concerned about the injured woman's ability to stay afloat, until the captain of the *Cariad* assured him she could.

The aircraft has a radar altimeter that shoots a signal to surface where it is bounced back to a receiver. The time it takes to make the round trip is calculated into altitude. The system can usually be programmed to hold a desired height, but in this instance with the seas running greater than 20 feet it was impossible. Bartlett had to continuously raise and lower the collective to stay at his desired altitude. Chris would have been unable to pay out and take up cable fast enough to keep pace with the up-and-down movement of the airframe. This made it vital for Bartlett to hold the correct altitude and position. Meader monitored the altitude gauge and called out varying disparities over the ICS.

Nor was this their only flying challenge. Based upon the weather report, Bartlett should have been able to nose the aircraft into the wind, obtain 45 knots of forward airspeed, and program the computer to hold it on that heading. He knew this was not the case. The wind swirled, pushed, pulled, gusted and slacked, and generally created an uncooperative frenzy. To control the helicopter Bartlett made constant adjustments of the cyclic, as if he were holding the handle of a spoon and stirring some unseen goo in the bottom of a bowl. Yet having repeatedly flown in these conditions, Bartlett gave the impression there was nothing to it.

Doug was in hand-to-hand combat with Mother Nature. Together the three-person crew of the *Cariad*, with life jackets on, had plunged into the sea. Doug powered through the waves like a freight train.

Calmly, but loudly, he yelled, "I'll put you one at a time into the basket."

Doug clamped a beefy arm across the chest of the female survivor and swam away from the two men, swimmers must gain clearance from multiple survivors to be sure the basket does not smack someone else or no more than one at a time attempts to enter it. This gives the swimmer a measure of control and allow for the safe rescue of all.

With blood still spilling from the woman's head, Doug wondered, not for the first time, if creatures higher on the food chain than the two of them would soon show up. Salt water spilled into his snorkel, and he swallowed it. Short choppy waves atop the rollers punched him as he swam. He gave the "Ready for Pickup" signal and waited for the basket.

At that point Chris was lying on the deck of the helicopter with the hoist-control handle in his left hand and the hoist cable in the other. He thumb-rolled the small wheel on the control handle and paid out slack while observing Doug and said, "Forward and right fifty feet."

Bartlett edged the aircraft closer to Doug while Chris tensed his muscles with every jerk of the cable and pushed the cable in the opposite direction to the basket's swing. This action counteracted the pendulum motion and gave Chris a measure of control. The basket slapped at the water to be pushed back, rolled on its side, and moved to a position under the tail. Doug, with leg muscles burning, kicked his finned feet uphill toward the rescue device, grabbed the rail of the basket with his left hand he and slid his charge inside its protective metal frame. He then released the woman from his left hand and reached around to grab the collar of her life jacket. Holding her in place, he shoved the rest of her body into the bottom of the basket with his chest. He had practiced this maneuver to polished quickness, so that hundredths of seconds after he had the basket in his hand he gave the thumbs-up signal.

"Keep your hands inside the basket," Doug screamed over the helicopter noise, a lesson survivors have learned the hard way. Unless they do so, a hand can slam into some portion of the airframe, and any limbs or digits extending beyond the protective metal of the basket are fair game.

"Ready for pickup. Taking up slack. Prepare to take the load," Chris announced over the ICS.

The cable rolled onto the drum above Chris's head as he retrieved it. As the basket cleared the water Doug held it with vise like fingers until it was as vertical as possible. This swimmer procedure is referred to as plumb and helps the flight mechanic control the swing. Once straight under the helicopter, Doug released and swam on his back away from the aircraft.

"Basket coming up, swimmer heading back toward the other survivors, clear back and left thirty," Chris said. By conning back and left, Bartlett could visually reacquire Doug and maintain correct position over the target, although most of his flying is done lost target.

"Cease commands," Bartlett said, telling Chris to take his eyes off the swimmer and concentrate on getting the basket inside.

"Roger, ceasing commands."

The basket bounced off the plastic skid plate mounted on the open door of the helicopter as the first of three survivors was pulled to safety.

Doug spun away from the hovering machine and met more walls of water. He did not see the two men, but he knew where he had left them and swam in that direction. On the crest of the next wave he spotted them and slightly altered his course for an intercept.

"Woman is out of basket, ready for another hoist," Chris said.

"Roger, begin the hoist."

The basket was outside the door and on its way down before Doug had reached the second man. "Who's next?" Doug asked the two remaining survivors like a drill sergeant addressing wayward recruits. The captain pointed toward the other man. "OK, let's go."

One at a time both men were plucked from the raging seas. Chris was about to go after Doug when he noticed something odd about the hoist hook.

"The hook clasp is bent," Chris explained to Bartlett.

"It won't lock closed. It must have happened when the sea was batting the basket around."

The hook has a hardened metal spring-loaded clasp that automatically closes and holds rescue devices on the cable. Now the twisting of the basket had bent the clasp and prevented it from functioning, with Doug still in the water.

Doug watched and waited as cold fingers of water crept inside his hood. He was tired and ready to go home.

After contemplating the risks of more hoists with a bent hook, Bartlett said, "Let's pickup Doug and take these survivors back to Elizabeth City instead of continuing on to the *Irish Mist*."

Chris let the thin steel cable slide through his hand as they moved to a position over Doug. "Swimmer approaching cable, swimmer has cable, prepare to take the load, taking the load." Chris hoisted Doug to the aircraft. "Swimmer's in the cabin, hoist complete."

"Randy, pass to the C-130 we will be returning to the air station. Let them know about the bent hoist hook and see if they have another part or another aircraft ready to go."

Thirty-eight minutes had elapsed from the first aborted hoist until Doug's final ride. The crew had saved three lives and had expended some of their available rescue energies, but not all. The physically demanding rescue of the crew of the *Cariad* had been straightforward and simple.

The final hoist of any rescue allows the aircrew to breathe a collective sigh of relief. Doug sat in the aircraft seat with water dripping from his dry suit and harness and visually checked the survivors. After a short rest he covered them with wool blankets and gathered personal information. Chris moved about the cabin and removed the leather hoist glove, stowed the rescue basket, and secured the cabin. Bartlett wrestled the weather for control of the aircraft as he turned toward shore. He noticed the rains had increased and were pounding the airframe.

It took them 45 minutes to reach the safety of the air station, and seconds before the wheels touched solid ground Meader received a call from the C-130.

"Three one from the O-four."

"O-four, this is the three one, go ahead."

"Roger, we have information on another boat in need of immediate assistance when you're ready to copy."

"Roger, send your traffic," Meader said as he pulled the pen from its slot on his kneeboard.

"The crew of the sailing boat *Hakuna Matata* is preparing to abandon ship. They are taking on water and are located sixty three miles offshore."

"Roger, we are on short final approach to E-City. We'll be airborne shortly and reestablish contact." After a moment he asked Bartlett, "Did you hear?"

"Yes, let's hurry."

When the crew radioed the Operation Center at the air station to advise that the hoist hook was bent, the duty watch officer immediately phoned the watch captain. The watch captain mustered the duty section, and they set about trying to solve the dilemma. Initially they tried to acquire a new hoist hook. As a backup plan they pulled a second helicopter from the hangar and fueled it to maximum capacity. Also, they filled the cabin with extra weight bags and trail lines just as they had with the first airframe.

The duty officer on the desk was in the middle of recalling a second crew, as it appeared that otherwise the crew of the *Irish Mist* might have to wait too long for a rescue.

Troy Lundgren, another rescue swimmer who lived just two minutes from the front gate of the air station, was first to respond to the order to report. He strode into the hangar shortly after the HH-60J had landed.

Troy, who has been described as a gladiator, possesses chiseled features, a muscular frame, and extraordinary athletic ability. He even played college football before choosing to become a rescue swimmer. His intimidating presence has served him well, for he eventually became a renowned instructor at the AST School in Elizabeth City.

By the time Troy met Doug on the hangar the crew of the *Cariad* had been moved from the helicopter to the waiting ambulance.

"How was it?" Troy asked Doug.

"Rough as shit."

"You guys want another swimmer on this next case?"

"I don't know about Bartlett, but I do. Let's ask him."

Bartlett was more than pleased to have two swimmers on board. His crew now numbered five.

The duty officer on the desk needed to call a third swimmer for the next set of pilots and flight mechanic to go after the *Irish Mist*.

Within 30 minutes Bartlett and his crew were airborne. Meader immediately established radio contact with the C-130. "One five zero four, this is the six zero two six."

"Two six from the O-four."

"Roger O-four, please pass updated position and condition of the *Hakuna Matata*."

"The *Hakuna Matata* is in close proximity to another boat also requesting assistance. The *Miss Manhattan* has a crew of five and they are preparing to abandon ship. They are about five miles from the *Hakuna Matata*."

Frustration might be a normal response for anyone not in this line of work. For the crew of Bartlett's HH-60J, the circumstances required quick and correct action. Triage is a term used by the emergency medical service community to determine life-saving priorities. On this day that task fell to Bartlett's shoulders, and he continued toward the *Hakuna Matata*.

"Plot a course to the *Hakuna Matata* and let's go on NVG's when we get the chance."

Meanwhile, back at the air station, Lcdr Randy Watson had arrived to hunker over the chart table making plans to go out to the *Irish Mist*. Not assigned duty, he had raced to the station when he received the call from the desk officer. Watson is tall, unflappable under pressure, and a soft-spoken pilot with a quiet passion for fast cars, with the rest of his crew on their way, he planned to launch as soon as they arrived.

The maintenance personnel hurriedly repaired the broken hoist hook on the 6031. This would be Watson's chariot.

In the HH-60J, tail number 6026, Meader received an update from the C-130. "Two six from the O four. The *Hakuna Matata* is crewed by a French father-son team. They do not speak very clear English, but the crew of the *Miss Manhattan* has been able to translate for us. They reported the *Matata* has experienced several knockdowns, which cracked their keel. They are taking on water and need immediate evacuation. We attempted to drop them a pump, but they were unable to get it started in these conditions."

The two sailboats were only miles apart, communicating and providing critical, invaluable information that was assisting in both their rescues.

"Randy, have the O-four drop a smoke pattern for our approach," Bartlett ordered. He was asking for a drop of three or more pyrotechnic flares into the water, upwind and angled off to one side of a hover target. These flares are saltwater activated and provide a small white flame and plume of smoke to alert the helicopter crew to the direction and strength of the surface winds, plus providing a solid hover reference. On a dark and stormy night the sky and sea can appear to melt into one black curtain, so that the pilot's eyes play tricks.

"Smokes are in the water," Meader reported in a moment.

"Roger that. Chris, complete part one."

Troy was strapped into the troop seat next to Doug. Bartlett had to decide which swimmer to use. He ordered Doug to prepare, assuming Troy would be fresh for later. Doug and Troy instinctively looked each other over, checking clasps for security to ensure that neither had forgotten a vital piece of gear. They shared excited smiles as adrenaline pumped through their veins.

By the time Bartlett was overhead of the *Hakuna Matata*, and Watson and his crew were airborne and en route to the *Irish Mist*. This lifted some of the burden from Bartlett's shoulders and let him concentrate on the two boats in trouble directly below his helicopter as he continued to communicate with the team.

"I'm going to pull into a hover just aft of the *Hakuna Matata* and plan on completing another rescue like before. Randy, relay through the translator on the *Miss Manhattan* that we want the crew of the

Matata to jump overboard when they see us deploy our swimmer into the water. Doug, you ready?"

"Oh, yeah!"

Bartlett peered out the right window at his shoulder. The hover light illuminated the rolling seas. The stage was dark; the sun had set. He could only see the area lit by the helicopter's hover lights but felt sure the well-rehearsed rescue would go as planned.

"Complete rescue check list part two."

"Roger, bringing swimmer aft."

Chris looked Doug over to be sure he had his fins and hadn't forgotten some vital piece of equipment, then rapped Doug's chest with a solid slap, at which point Doug gave the ready for hoist signal.

"Swimmer's ready."

"Roger, begin the hoist."

"Swimmer is going up and out the door," Chris said. "Swimmer holding, waiting on load check," he watched for Doug's second thumb-up signal.

"Load check good, swimmer going down." Chris rolled the thumb wheel on the hoist control pendant, and the tightly woven steel cable peeled off the drum.

The steady howl of the wind mixed with the scream of the helicopter. The *Hakuna Matata* was closer to the center of the low-pressure system. The winds blew a steady 50 knots and created seas in excess of 30 feet, blue-black rollers the height of three-story buildings, unforgiving and powerful.

"Swimmer's in the water, paying out slack."

"Here comes a big one." Meader was looking toward the lit horizon, and Bartlett pulled power to lift the aircraft above the crest of the wave.

"Swimmer's away." Several seconds passed. "Swimmer's OK."

Bartlett backed the helicopter rearward to watch Doug, as the survivors hurled themselves into the sea from the floundering *Hakuna Matata*.

Doug's muscles screamed with effort as he battled a ceaseless onslaught from the waves. The helicopter's spotlight bounced around so that it gave only split-second warnings on any advancing wave, and each time Doug saw a wave it was almost upon him. Water slammed his torso, filled his mouth and his snorkel, forcing him to swallow it.

Pounding Doug's body like a punching bag, the sea dealt him one blow after another.

The crew of the *Hakuna Matata* struggled to survive themselves, wide eyed and terrified as they watched Doug swim over the crest of wave after wave to inch toward them.

Undaunted, Doug twisted his head to the side to vomit then brought his eyes forward in one smooth motion. The queasiness did not deter him.

"Swimmer has first survivor," Chris said.

"I have ready for pick up signal."

"Roger that, conn me in."

"Forward and right twenty feet."

Bartlett flicked the trim tap on the cyclic up and to the right. Each single push of the small moon-shaped button normally moved the hovering aircraft five feet in the direction indicated. Bartlett was still stirring the bowl and had to constantly adjust the flight controls to move the airframe in the desired heading. The winds remained steady at 50 knots with occasional gust to 60.

Bartlett concentrated on the bobbing flares visible now and then atop the passing waves.

"Up, Up," Meader said as a rogue wave approached.

Bartlett lifted the collective causing the helicopter to ascend.

Doug struggled toward the basket, only to be attacked from behind. The cresting, breaking wave rolled Doug and his survivor underwater. When he looked for light to swim toward, he saw none. The air in his lungs burned to exit, yet he knew that to breathe was to drown, not an option. Instead, Doug kept his powerful arm locked across the chest of the man who was trusting him with his very life. Doug's throat started to constrict and convulse as his body responded to the desire to gasp. Still underwater, he had to wait for relief of the wave's release. At last, though, as the sea spit the two men to the surface like a mouthful of rancid milk, they sucked oxygen, to reclaim their hold on life. Doug looked around and for the first time in his life felt his own mortality.

"Need a little help down here, God," Doug silently prayed as he looked around to gain his bearings. He needed to finish this hoist before another wave sucker-punched him.

Chris spotted Doug popping to the surface and dropped the

basket within five feet of him. Doug was still a little dazed when he realized the basket was merely a few feet from his grasp.

"Swimmer has the basket."

"Survivor's in the basket, taking up slack, prepare to take the load, taking the load, basket is clear of the water, clear back and left." Chris's steady stream of information painted a clear picture of all that Bartlett could not see.

Bartlett backed away until Doug's stroking arms came into view. Doug was already flying through the water toward the second man.

"Uuuurrraa!" Doug vomited again, then took a mouthful of salt water to wash the taste away.

The second hoist was smoother than the first. Thirty-three minutes had elapsed by the time the second survivor was inside the helicopter and Doug had joined them—two more lives saved.

"Good job everybody," Bartlett said. "Now let's finish this. Troy you ready?" Bartlett was watching the lights on the horizon where the *Miss Manhattan* and her crew of five waited.

"Randy, have the fifteen O-four drop some more smokes in the vicinity of the *Miss Manhattan.*"

"They are running low on fuel and will have to depart scene soon," Meader reported. "They said they would drop the flares before heading to the barn. And Rick, the crew of the *Manhattan* is still trying to decide whether to abandon ship."

Bartlett continued flying toward the *Manhattan*. "I've got two cold, wet survivors, and a C-one thirty departing scene. They need to decide now or wait on the six zero two six to return from the rescue of the crew of the *Irish Mist.*"

As the crew of the *Manhattan* digested Bartlett's words, a wall of water higher than 30 feet heaved the sailboat toward the heavens, then rolled and stabbed its mast into the Atlantic. For several seconds that seemed like a lifetime, the mast remained buried in the churning blue-black water, and when the *Manhattan* finally righted herself, thousands of gallons of water poured from the cockpit.

An unidentified female voice screamed over the radio: "We're ready to come off—right now!"

"Complete part one for sling deployment of the swimmer," Bartlett ordered. "Randy, call the crew, let's continue to use what's been working. Have them jump from the boat when they see our swimmer enter the water."

Meader was talking on the radio while Troy spit into his mask to keep it from fogging and climbed onto the deck. He attached the gunner's belt around his waist, then Chris handed Troy the hoist hook and motioned him to slide toward the open door.

"Swimmer's in the door, ready for sling deployment."

Troy had been a spectator until now. The wind had gathered strength during the passing minutes until it sounded like the steady blast of a train whistle. Bucketfuls of rain sloshed sideways in front of his eyes in what seemed like a solid wall of water. The airframe was jolted roughly while he looked down at the *Miss Manhattan*.

Troy, like every other adrenalin-charged rescue swimmer, relished the sensation of the solid open-palm slap on his chest and removed the gunner's belt.

"Swimmers ready."

Chris sharply eyed Troy's equipment before pushing the thumb wheel upward, taking slack from the cable and hefting Troy from the deck as he made adjustments to the harness. He automatically gave the second thumbs-up as he concentrated on the seas below him. They appeared to be rising, but he knew he was being lowered toward them, to be tackled the moment he hit the water. When he released the hook the next wave pushed and rolled him over. Nausea seized over him as he swam; still he gave the "I'm all right" signal.

Black and gray in the light of the helicopter the water seemed alive with vicious intent. Small rain driven bullets of water sprang from the surface as the wave tops burst to skirt just above the water.

The force he faced at that moment, would call on every ounce of Troy's strength. Belching as he swam he knew this was only the beginning of his body's reaction to the motion of the sea, and soon he vomited with force. "Just getting started, can't quit now," he thought.

The crew of the *Miss Manhattan* splashed haplessly into the ocean, but not all at once and not together. Troy swam toward the closest one.

"Just relax," he said. "We do this all the time. We'll have you out of here in a second."

Troy locked his arm across the chest of the woman and turned toward the lights of the helicopter. It seemed a greater swim back than it had been on the way out. The chopper bounced wildly, and occasionally he lost sight of it below the wave tops, but he could hear the scream of the engines and continued to swim closer to the pickup point.

From the door of the helicopter Chris watched Troy give the ready for pickup signal.

"Basket holding ten feet off the water, forward and right fifteen feet,"

Bartlett gave no verbal response, but the airframe inched closer and Chris lowered the basket to splash into the water.

"Swimmer has the basket, he's throwing up, but is giving the ready for pickup signal."

The flight mechanic is required to provide both conning commands and advisories, information vital to the aircraft commander's flying decisions. How tired is the swimmer? Is the rescue equipment functioning normally? If over a boat, is the cable in danger of becoming entangled? In this instance Bartlett worried about Troy becoming dehydrated, particularly in view the long distances needed to reach and recover each survivor. It was a hell of a swim in such conditions.

Troy hung onto the basket until it was yanked from the waves, then turned back to continue his effort. His vomiting became regular and violent, yet he ignored it and swam toward survivor number two.

By the time he had number three on the way up Bartlett had decided to pull Troy from the water. The two remaining survivors had drifted farther apart, and Troy's seasickness had not let up. Unable to talk directly to Troy to ask about his physical condition, instead he called on his other swimmer.

"Doug, are you rested and ready to give Troy a break?"

"Yes sir."

"Chris, let's complete a bare-hook recovery of the swimmer, then prepare to deploy Doug."

"Roger, bare hook going down."

Grateful for the reprieve, Troy climbed inside the helicopter and tilted his head against the windowsill. Even then his dizziness and queasiness did not subside.

For Doug, the sight of Troy's sickness and the motion of the water quickly brought back the knot in his stomach. "Only two left, then we can go home," he thought.

"Randy, have the O-four contact the six zero two three one," Bartlett directed. "If they have finished with their rescue of the crew of the *Irish Mist*, I am requesting they stand by as our backup. If we can't finish this, I want them here to help."

Meador began talking on the radio while Bartlett and Chris returned their attention to the water and Doug. By now Doug had fought his way to the last two survivors who clutched desperately to an uninflated but still floating life raft.

"I'll take one at a time just like the others. Keep your hands and feet inside the basket," Doug explained as he always did, but got no response from either man. As EMTs we are trained to recognize and treat hypothermia in our patients, and it appeared to Doug that these two had been in the water long enough to reach that lethargic and confused state. He needed to act quickly as they were close to death.

Doug pried the cold stiff fingers of one of the men from the raft and turned toward the basket. It was coming into view as soon as he hustled toward the helicopter. As Doug swam, the waves attacked again.

"I can't see those damn things coming" he thought as he and his survivor were rolled underwater. "Come on, God, air please," he prayed.

They found the surface immediately and the basket was within reach. Doug slung the heavy man inside the bails of the rescue device but had to wrestle with the man's lethargic legs to force them to follow. He then spun around to return for the last man. The sounds of the sea were overwhelming. Seeing the waves coming his way was bad enough; hearing them coming was worse.

"I got you," Doug screamed into the unresponsive man's ear upon reaching him. With renewed energy, Doug kicked his finned feet as his leg muscles screamed for relief. He tried to outswim the next wave, to no avail. It caught him just as he reached for the basket.

"Oh shit!" he gasped for air as he and the survivor were dragged under the white foamy expanse. This wave was the worst, and it carried them deep. He spit the snorkel mouthpiece from his lips and gritted his teeth against the urge to breathe.

"Hold on," he thought toward the man still wrapped in his arm. This will be over soon, one way or the other. Doug was about to give up and take a deep gulp of water when they popped to the surface. He turned and powered back toward the basket.

Onboard the aircraft Chris said, "Swimmer is at the six o-clock, back twenty feet."

Doug contorted the near-frozen man's body and forced him inside the basket, then rolled onto his stomach and looked for the next wave, determined to not be surprised again. Within seconds Chris had tipped the basket over and dropped the survivor to the deck of the airframe. Troy then dragged the man from the device, and Chris swung it back outside the door.

Chris reported, "Basket outside the cabin door, going down. Hold your position, swimmer at three o-clock, zero feet."

Doug smiled. "I'm outta here," he said to no one, then clambered into the basket before it was fully immersed. The ocean threw one last rogue wave at him, slamming into the metal device and spinning it upside down. Doug clamped onto the rails and took a deep breath, when the feeling of being yanked skyward erased his sensation of being upside down.

Chris was smiling. "Swimmer's clear of the water, basket is coming up."

Bartlett, Meador, Chris, Doug, and Troy were done. Chris closed the door of their helicopter at 11:11 PM. They had been flying for 5 ½ hours, three of them were in a hover in nasty winter storm conditions. They had saved a total of ten lives.

〰

Yet another account of what happened that night was shared by, Shannon Scaff, a rescue swimmer assigned to my shop. His aircraft commander was Lcdr Watson.

Watson assembled his crew at the door of the HH-60J, and as always his highly polished boots, seamlessly smooth flight suit, and above-average preparedness elicited respect from those privileged to know him.

Before they crawled into the belly of the fish-shaped aircraft with its distinctive red and blue stripes, Watson addressed his crew. "The weather is worse offshore than it is here. Bartlett and his men have their hands full. We're going after a boat called the *Irish Mist*. It has two crew and a dog and has taken a pounding for the past several hours. From what I've heard, we will be unable to hoist from the deck of the boat, it's too rough out there. We will adhere to standard procedures throughout and you are *required* to speak up if something is not going as you think it should. We'll stop and talk about it at that point."

Watson's requirement to voice an opinion was a radical departure from the mindset of aircraft commanders of the past. The earlier ones had almost been revered as demigods whose word was never questioned, a notion Watson threw out the window. Doing so enabled him to reach a level of expertise that those before him had not been able to obtain.

Shannon Scaff was the third rescue swimmer to be called in that night. Shannon knew Troy and Doug were in the middle of a difficult rescue, and he felt the initial surge of adrenaline as he listened to Watson. Shannon oozed confidence from every pore, a man who never imagined he might fail to complete a rescue. Anyone hoping to navigate the modern-day rescue swimmer school must posses a determined spirit, and I tell those on the waiting list they must be willing to die rather than give up, for if they lack this trait they will not make it through the training.

Watson's crew gathered in front of Maintenance Control, a small office close to the large hangar doors which is the nerve center for the watch captain and the rest of the duty section.

Adam Sustachek adjusted the survival vest he had taken from the wood locker on the hangar deck as Watson spoke. An exceptionally good mechanic Adam had worked on every airframe system, with the exception of avionics, when not performing the duties of flight mechanic. He kept his blond hair as long and wavy as regulations allowed and ditched the thick, black-rimmed, Coast Guard issued eyeglasses for a more modern pair. Adam smiled nervously as he waited to board the helicopter.

The other member of the crew was Lt Nick Koester. Dark haired with a straightforward demeanor, he was a capable aircraft commander in his own right. All Coast Guard HH-60J aircraft have a minimum of two pilots.

Before I became immersed in the world of Coast Guard aviation the question of how pilots became proficient at flying in horrific conditions never occurred to me. I learned they become excellent stick jockeys because of the leadership of those flying with them. In this case Watson asked, "Nick, do you want the right seat?" This seemingly benign question revealed how pilots are transformed into seasoned veterans. Watson was relinquishing the coveted right pilot seat to Koester. Although Koester was already an aircraft commander, he had never faced the conditions they flew into that night. By sitting in the right seat Koester became the pilot in control, the decision maker, in essence—The Man. "Sure," he said.

The crew had no questions at the end of the brief. They stormed from the hangar and hustled toward the helicopter that the line crew had already towed onto the ramp.

By 10:53 PM Koester had the HH-60J, tail number 6031, bouncing along the same course Bartlett had attempted earlier. Unlike Bartlett's crew, they were not ordered to change course. By 11:25 PM they circled above the much-maligned *Irish Mist*.

"What's your on scene weather," the radioman from the 1504 asked. One of the benefits of having a high-flying eye in the sky is the ability to assist with communications when we might otherwise be out of range.

Watson said, "Ceiling is about three hundred feet. Visibility is two and a half and winds are from zero two zero degrees at steady fifty knots with gusts to sixty. Seas are running," he paused to look outside the window, "a steady thirty feet."

Koester asked, "Shannon, if we deploy you in the water behind the boat, do you think you can grab the line trailing behind the boat and pull yourself on?"

"No problem," Shannon said. Neither man realized Bartlett and his crew had attempted the same thing without success. If they had, it might have swayed their decision. They followed the same steps as Bartlett's crew and ended with the same results. Shannon had to be recovered after several fruitless minutes of powerful swimming effort.

Koester said, "Well that didn't work. Let's have the crew enter the water once we place Shannon in. Sound good?"

"Works for me." Shannon bent close to the window glass next to his radio console on the left side of the aircraft. Even at 300 feet he could see the seas rolling beneath the aircraft like giant killers, indifferent to their victims. Mother Nature has many children, and that night she let some of her nastiest come out to play.

Shannon signaled Adam with a thumb-up before he slid to the deck and attached the gunner's belt. He was then lifted from the dark gray deck of the helicopter into a black-gray night. He adjusted the lifting straps of the Tri-SAR harness and gave Adam the second required thumb-up. Almost immediately the wind assaulted Shannon once he was lowered below the bottom of the airframe. He felt the pressure and power Troy and Doug had surely experienced themselves, miles away.

Shannon entered the water to the sensation of stepping in front of a runaway freight train. As a towering wave slapped his skin and stung his face with its cold power, he reached up and released his harness from the hoist hook. The freedom was a relief, the responsibility heavy. He turned toward the *Irish Mist* and watched the male crewmember jump with the family dog in his arms. Dogs are not our problem, but we will rescue them given the chance if it does not interfere with saving human lives, and a dog alone in the middle of a storm like this is surely a dead dog. The female crewman stayed on the boat to provide steerage, and keep the boat away from the hoisting site. In the water man and dog faced Shannon and squinted against the stabbing rain and oxygen-sucking waves.

Shannon's training and adrenaline kicked in simultaneously. He sprinted through the water hard and fast. Years earlier he had lost the pinky of his left hand in an accident on a Coast Guard cutter, and sometimes the flopping pinky finger of his glove will serve to distract survivors from panic long enough for Shannon to approach without that complication. He can see the thought process in their eyes: "Did he break his finger? Is he ignoring the pain to come after us?"

On this night, though, there were too many distractions to worry about, and Shannon grabbed the man as soon as he reached him.

"Does the dog bite?" he asked the man in the water. If so he had no intention of allowing it in the aircraft. A really angry dog could conceivably cause the aircraft to crash, or at least cause bodily harm to the crew in the back, and that he would not allow.

"No..no.. he won't bite," the man gasped in a thick Australian accent

"OK, hold onto him tight. I'm going to take both of you to the basket. And don't worry, we do this all the time." Shannon had noticed the concerned look on the man's face.

Adam was already rocketing the basket downward when Shannon turned to give the ready for pickup signal. A split second later the basket bounced across the wave top and settled calmly in the water. Shannon wrenched the rescue device from the sliding face of the wave and brought it close to man and dog, awkwardly struggling to push both of them into the basket at once. The smooth practiced effort swimmers normally use did not work. It took too long. As Shannon wrestled with the basket and man and dog, an unexpected wave pushed them all under. As in the attacks on Doug and Troy, Shannon was hit from behind. The wave curled and broke across the surface, rolling the water back onto itself. Close to the beach, surfers might have rushed a curl like this for a ride of a lifetime. For Shannon, it flipped the three of them over and for a second sent them sailing through the air, then the water-saturated air exploded back into the sea and finally slammed them into the wave's trough. The powerful impact shot all three in different directions. Twisted and turned underwater by the surge of pure power, Shannon screamed inwardly, "Damn it, damn it! Where are they?" He turned and saw nothing but moving blackness. He kicked and kicked, swimming in no particular direction, confident that the buoyancy of his equipment would eventually bring him to the surface, where he needed to be. He had to find the man. It was his job.

At last the floodlight of the aircraft illuminated the man's flailing arms in the foamy seas. Shannon saw him immediately and powered toward the survivor, realizing that the dog was swimming in circles out of reach. After regaining control of his first survivor he leaned onto his back and gave Adam the ready for pickup signal. The basket was already below the aircraft and coming toward them as Lt Koester coaxed the aircraft in Shannon's direction.

"MY DOG!" the man screamed.

"I'll get him," Shannon promised, not sure he could carry through.

The basket landed with a splash next to them, and Shannon loosened his grip across the man's chest, rolled the man inside the bails of the basket, and held him there to give Adam a thumb-up signal. He felt the cable go tight and prayed it would clear the water before another wave hit them. Adam rolled the thumb wheel on the hoist-control handle to its full up position, causing the hoist to suck cable into the drum at a rate of 250 feet per minute. This maneuver, called two blocking, can be a rough ride, but it also can be effective.

As soon as the man was above the waves, Shannon spun around, feeling queasy from swallowing saltwater. Ignoring the churning in the pit of his stomach, he searched for the *Irish Mist* through 360 degrees without finding the boat and his last survivor. The boat had disappeared, but still swimming in circles just 25 yards away, he spotted the dog.

"They will be a minute before they pick me up, so I might as well see if I can catch this mutt,'" Shannon thought, approaching cautiously not knowing what to expect. Even the tamest of dogs might become violent in such circumstances. This dog was a healthy-sized yellow Lab with terror filled eyes, but once Shannon moved to face it, the dog settled its paws on his shoulders and relaxed to let Shannon hold its weight in the water.

"It's OK, boy, we'll get you out of here," he said.

"Shannon has the dog," Adam said as the survivor crawled from the basket.

"I see that, let's pick him up," Koester ordered.

"Conn me in."

"Forward and right, fifty feet, basket's going down."

"See, here it comes," Shannon explained to the dog as the basket came into view of the hover lights. The metal rescue device landed with a gentle splash. Adam paid out enough slack to allow the basket to ride the backside of the wave, and Shannon settled the dog feet first in the bottom of the basket. The Lab seemed to know not to climb out and crouched low, shakily but still, as it waited. Shannon gave the ready for pickup signal. Adam rolled the cable up until the basket shot from the sea.

"Basket is clear of the water, clear to move back and left thirty."

"Roger, once that dog is inside leave it in the basket and send the bare hook down for Shannon. We need to reposition to pick up our final survivor."

Watson had monitored the forward progress of the *Irish Mist* and knew they would have to move Shannon closer. He let Koester know the boat was in forward motion, and they agreed they needed to reposition Shannon. Adam lowered the bare hoist hook to Shannon, who knew he was to be hoisted and, most likely, moved closer to the boat.

"Swimmer attaching the hook, prepare to take the load."

Shannon was hoisted into the cabin and Koester hover-taxied the aircraft aft of the sailboat. They followed the same steps they had used earlier and Shannon again found himself in the maelstrom of the Atlantic. Gratefully, the woman abandoned the wounded sailboat's wheel.

Shannon told her, "That last hoist was a little rough, so I'm going to lock my hands around you. If we go for a ride underwater, just hold your breath and relax, we will come back to the surface in short order." He was relieved to be rid of the dog, having almost lost a human being while trying to save it.

Shannon gave the signal and swam toward the downward spiral of light coming from the underside of the helicopter, looking up to watch the gleaming black letters USCG on its white underbelly grow larger.

"Forward and right ten feet," Adam conned.

"Roger, lost target."

"Swimmer approaching basket, swimmer has the basket, waiting for ready for pickup signal."

"Have ready for pickup, taking up slack, prepare to take the load, taking the load," Adam said as he hoisted the basket from the water.

"I've got to get out of here," Shannon thought as his seasickness returned with a vengeance. The bare hook descending was a welcome sight.

"Swimmer has the hook, is connecting the hook. Have the ready for pickup signal. Swimmer's inside the cabin, hoist complete."

Watson, monitoring the radios, said, "The six zero two six has requested we cover them in case they can't retrieve everyone from the two boats they are hoisting from." There was no time to celebrate. If another crew was requesting assistance, they needed to hurry.

"One five O-four, advise the two six we are en route to their position," Koester reported.

"Nice job gentlemen, Now let's give our brothers whatever help they need," Watson said over the ICS.

At 12:40 AM on 30 May, Koester added power, tilted the nose over, and headed toward Bartlett and the crew of the crew of the 6026.

As it turned out, Bartlett and crew needed no assistance. Later, both aircrews assembled at the hangar to discuss the events of the past few hours, in detail, with many congratulations passed out. They had saved the lives of twelve sailors and one dog. All aircrews had returned safely, and no aircraft were damaged. Bartlett's thought Chris, his flight mechanic, summed the whole thing up well: "It was a good night."

CHAPTER 14

Katrina

In the wake of Hurricane Katrina in 2005, Lake Pontchartrain escaped confinement to bury the city of New Orleans under fifteen feet of water. Twenty hours after the levees broke I was in the open door of a Coast Guard HH-60J, wind whipping my face, racing toward the unknown. Fourteen years had passed since I last saw the city, and the first signs of what Katrina had done twisted my stomach into knots.

It was late afternoon on Wednesday 31 August 2005, and AST2 Scott Rady and I were wearing our shorty wet suits, sweating in the heat and humidity. I have known Scott for ten years and have confidence in his abilities, after helping him qualify as a rescue swimmer and seeing him in action. He is solid and tough. His knotty muscles rippled as he tensed at the sights below us. The water was up to the eaves of many houses; we saw shingled islands extend to the horizon. Except where our rotor wash made waves, the air was calm and the water still. This was not destruction by wind and sea, but a city drowned.

Our flight to New Orleans had carried us over cement slabs where houses had once withstood the fury of Camille, but not Katrina. Gambling ships four and five stories tall and hundreds of feet long were tossed ashore like toys. Piles of raw lumber, all that was left of people's homes, formed roadblocks and covered every inch of soil. Highways were torn away from their foundations and pilings. Entire cities were gone. It was beyond belief.

Inside the aircraft I felt a mix of quiet resolve and barely controlled adrenaline. I locked my jaw and leaned over to Scott, lifted my helmet microphone, and yelled, "You take the first one." This was Scott's second sortie into the rescue zone, and I thought it might be like the aftermath of Hurricane Floyd in 1999. I had been stationed in Elizabeth City, North Carolina when that storm came ashore to flood the Tar River Basin. If the aftermath of this storm was similar, we would both see our share of rescues.

I had known our pilots, Lcdr Jim Fergenson and Lcdr Chris Conley, for years and was glad to have two experienced sticks flying the aircraft. While it is rare to fly with two swimmers, in this case the pilots thought it would be useful, so Scott and I piled into their aircraft and took off from Mobile, Alabama.

"Our mission is to fly into the flood zone and save lives. Any questions?" Conley asked. We had none.

Once we had reached the edge of the flood zone they jumped the helicopter down low, avoiding power lines and trees, and picked a rooftop with two survivors at random. After Scott took the offered hoist hook from the flight mechanic, AMT2 S.J. Conrad, and attached his harness, Conrad lowered him smoothly to the first roof where Scott quickly disconnected. He hustled over to the survivors, who had rolled into the fetal position to protect themselves from the rotor wash. As if calling a touchdown, he signaled for the rescue basket with two upright arms. Minutes later the two survivors and Scott were safely back inside the aircraft, and the pilots hover-taxied to the next roof—and the next and the next.

Scott and I took turns rescuing survivors until we happened upon a skeleton of an office building under construction. We saw several people inside the metal girders and stringers but could not determine how many, and they were trapped one floor below the roof. I offered to go down and find a solution and in seconds was hanging from the clothesline-thin hoist cable. Roofing rocks, as fine as grains of sands, were whipped into a tornado and loose construction material blew back and forth. Once on deck and free from the hook I raised my arm above my head and held a palm upward, the signal for "I am OK" and walked over to a gap between the part of the roof I was on and another level covering the rest of the building. When I poked my head through, I saw several people twenty feet below me.

"How many are there?" I asked.

"Six, but one just swam off."

I had my radio tucked in the pocket of my harness with a remote microphone snapped to the harness riser on my right shoulder. I keyed the mike and asked for Scott to be hoisted down and explained the challenge with bringing the survivors to the roof. As the building was in the beginning stages of construction, no stairs, elevators, or other means of ascent were in place. I surmised they had initially swum to the second floor, as the water was just below that level.

"Sit tight," I yelled down before leaving them to look for a way up.

The building was three stories tall, about the length of a football field. Scott landed with a solid thud and hustled over when I found a construction ladder leaning up through an access hole in the deck at the far end.

"Call for a basket and I'll bring them to you," I said then went down one floor.

All five survivors had a bag of possessions, some had trash bags, and others had suitcases. I considered this for a minute. "If we took their bags that would preempt space we could use to get more survivors. On the other hand if I had just lost everything else, I'd cling to what little I had left." I helped them bring their bags up with them. I almost lost the first survivor, a tall, fit-looking man of about fifty, when his weight shifted the ladder, so I tied the ladder down to the rail with some rope from a pile of building materials. The rest followed one at a time. This was the first time Scott and I had worked a roof together and we were faster together than alone, a thought I held on to.

The entire aircrew was getting into a rhythm as we worked the rooftops. We came upon one family of eight trapped on their second-floor balcony. Water lapped the wooden deck, and an oak tree blocked enough of that to prevent us from hoisting to it.

This was the first time we were simultaneously hoisted together. A standard procedure is delivering one of us to a rescue target while still on our harness. In addition, our harnesses allow us to retrieve another person who happens to be wearing one, such a military aviator or another swimmer by connecting to theirs. But we have no procedure for delivering two swimmers to a target, and because we rarely fly more than one swimmer in an aircraft this was an untested method. I don't remember whose idea it was, but seemed like a time-saver and we decided it would work. We were improvising.

At the time we didn't have a name for this new delivery method, but as it became the norm for Katrina rooftop rescues I heard it called many things. The two swimmers are being hoisted so close together that I suspect AST3 Matt Novellino referred to it as the Reverse Double Direct Heterosexual Swimmer Deployment to reassert our manliness. The name I like best, though, Double Direct Delivery was widely used during Katrina rescues, whether or not it becomes an option for future aircrews.

At Scott's urging, having learned from his previous day's experience, we aimed for and landed on the peak of the roof. He had learned the hard way that you can't always determine roof steepness when hovering above it, and the rotor wash can easily knock you over. We disconnected and in concert lifted our open palms to the sky.

Scott had also learned one more important lesson that I was just catching on to. He was wearing his regular flight boots instead of his wetsuit booties. My feet were sweating, like the rest of me, and I found it difficult to keep a sure footing on the asphalt shingles. Scott paced ahead of me and never slowed as he jumped off the roof with his arms splayed wide to sail to the deck below. He absorbed the shock by dropping to his knees as he landed, then stood up and faced the wide eyes of our survivors and asked if they were injured.

"There is an old lady next door trapped in the water up to her neck," a young man of about twelve years old told him. He had swum some food and water to her and returned just before we arrived. Scott and I decided to rescue this family now and let the pilots know about the woman once we were back inside the helicopter.

This family had two adults and six children, two of them still in diapers. Scott looked around for a way of getting them to the roof and found a small metal ladder hanging in the branches of the oak tree. When he grabbed it and leaned it against the eave, it proved too short, and the children were too small to climb it. So the mom clambered up as Scott handed me one of the toddlers, then with the child clinging to my neck I signaled for the basket and turned to grab the second child as Scott passed her to me. I walked the three of them up to the peak of the roof and said, "Kneel down and hold onto me."

The noise of the helicopter was deafening, and the wind pounded at our bodies as the basket landed with a thud.

Scott and I worked together like this until all eight survivors were safely inside the aircraft. We were hoisted together via our harnesses in a traditional double lift.

Our aircraft cabin, which is about six feet wide, twelve feet long, and five feet high, was packed with survivors. Some had smiles, other had tears, and the youngest was asleep, having screamed himself to exhaustion. Conley added power and the helicopter shuddered higher, on our way to deliver them to the Cloverleaf, a designated spot on Interstate 10 where help was supposed to be waiting. I connected to the ISC and told the pilots about the elderly lady trapped in the water and asked them to mark the position in the navigation computer.

By the time we had returned to the same area, darkness had engulfed the city and the lights flashing from the rooftops looked like twinkling stars. Using a distinctive, mostly submerged, dump truck as a visual aid, we relocated the exact home we had hoisted our last family from. Conley moved over one roof expecting to find our elderly lady and dropped Scott down, picked up two more survivors, and quickly learned we had missed the house with by one roof. Deftly Conley moved the hovering aircraft over the correct one.

With the overwhelming number of survivors needing rescue we were constantly brainstorming about ways to speed our progress. The faster and more clearly we communicated with each other, the more people we could rescue. Before I was hoisted to the next house we had devised a hand signal to indicate that the swimmer on the deck needed the second swimmer's assistance; I was to look up and rotate my arms as if swimming.

The flight mechanic, S.J. Conrad, smoothly lowered me to the flat-topped roof of a duplex apartment. I wasn't sure how I was going to extricate the woman from the flooded building, so I had brought an aircraft crash ax down with me, a resource ingrained in me from the flood rescues I participated in after Floyd. I already had one packed in my swimmer gear bag.

"Anybody home?" I yelled over the helicopter noise, while moving around the roof edge looking down to each window. Initially I heard no answer, but soon I saw her head as she peeked up from a window on the front of the building. I looked up and gave the second swimmer signal.

An oak tree blocking the window was thrashing about from the rotor wash. Once Scott was on the roof with me, we looked at the tree, thickness of the roof, and the difficulty of climbing down to the window and decided a direct deployment, a procedure where I stay on the hoist hook, would be our best option. I would then rappel to another window not blocked by the tree. I called the helicopter on the radio to discuss our new plan.

"How much room do you have from that tree?" they asked.

I knew we only had about five feet of clearance.

"You've got at least ten feet," I yelled to ensure that my voice carried over the hovering aircraft noise.

"I'm not sure that's enough room."

"We can do this, no problem."

I grabbed the hook as it touched the roof and soon I was hanging hoist cable over the side of the building, straddling the partially open window. I then wedged the blade of the ax inside and forced it wide enough to squeeze through.

Finally we had found our target, nervously pacing back and forth, trapped on the second floor with the water to the top of her stairs and rising. She was not, as originally reported, up to her neck in water, but she was definitely in need of immediate rescue.

"My friend is dead downstairs. I want to leave and never come back," she said in a strong voice.

While she was talking I looked around the cluttered room for a way out, to find none. I prodded the edges of the window with my ax, testing how hard it might be to remove it. I didn't want to have to hoist through broken glass, and the opening was too small for the basket. When the wood gave a little under my pressure, I let adrenaline take control and released a full-stroke swing, then several more, busting out the window, wood frame, and a small part of the wall. Scott was on the roof looking down, and I yelled up for him to signal for the basket and hand it down to me once he had it.

As Scott moved off to receive the basket I ducked back inside, sweat pouring off me, still working the angles of the rescue in my mind. At around five feet tall my survivor was too small to climb onto what was left of the windowsill. I grabbed a nightstand and turned it on its side underneath the window.

"We'll get you up on the nightstand, onto the window ledge, and into the basket. Are you ready?"

She nodded.

I climbed back up onto the sill and took the basket from Scott. It was still attached to the hoist cable. This was the most dangerous part of the rescue. Conrad, operating the hoist, could not see the basket, and I could not see what the aircraft was doing. We both hoped nothing went wrong for the next thirty seconds.

My survivor tried, but could not climb up high enough. I moved around behind her, gently lifted her in my arms, stepped up on the nightstand, and placed her in the basket. Then I poked my head out the window and gave Scott the thumbs up, which he relayed to Conrad. Very slowly the slack in the hoist cable disappeared, as I pushed her out into open air, and up she went.

As our survivor went up Scott was tending the trail line, a polypropylene line 105 feet long that we use to control the swing and spin of rescue devices. Once she was inside the aircraft he returned to the window and helped pull me up. A double lift later, and we were on to the next rescue.

Later, with a dozen people stuffed in the cramped cabin, we spotted an apartment complex full of survivors. They had hacked a hole through the third-floor roof and were waving at us with a flashlight.

By now our standard methods of hand signals and hoisting had become comfortable. I was sent down to investigate via my harness. When survivors began crawling up through the hole, I saw that things could get out of hand quickly. I signaled for Scott to join me and went to talk to the apparent leader—the guy with the light. He might have been New Orleans Police or just someone wearing a NOPD tee-shirt. Either way, he was frantic to call a loved one and let her know he was all right. If I had had my cell phone I would have loaned it to him. My mind focused on the task at hand.

"How many in this building?"

"I don't know, twenty-five, maybe one hundred."

More heads popped up through the hole as I listened. We needed some control to prevent someone from being blown off the roof and to stave off panic. Scott was disconnecting from the hook when I realized we were not going to be able to rescue everyone. There were just too many.

When Scott reached me I told him, "I'm going to find as many elderly and sick as possible. Find out how many we can take."

I saw but couldn't hear Scott talking on his radio as I descended into the hole. Once down in the rafters I saw nothing but grim faces with expectant expressions.

"Man, there are a lot of people down here," I thought.

"Send me the sick, injured, women, and children," I said as I climbed down farther. A medium-framed young man, probably in his early twenties, jumped to within inches of my face.

"THERE IS A FOUR-HUNDRED-POUND WOMAN DOWN THERE. WHAT ARE YOU GOING TO DO ABOUT IT?" he screamed, repeating himself twice more and getting louder and closer with each refrain. I thought he might be high, as he seemed to be behaving outside the norm. But, none of us had ever witnessed something like this, so he could have simply been scared out of his mind and expressing it.

"Step back right now!" I demanded with authority and he did, calming himself as he moved aside. I looked back toward the opening, and Scott reminded me to stay on the beams. We had heard that hours earlier another swimmer had fallen through the drywall ceiling, a mistake we did not want to repeat. Scott's legs dangled in the hole as he waited on whomever I sent him. Within moments I had four young women standing in front of me, covered in drywall dust and insulation, and I guided them up to Scott who lifted them to the roof. We only had room for four more survivors, and I had to break the news to those we had to leave behind, including that 400 pound woman trapped below.

"Keep waving your light at the helicopters. There are a bunch of them out here, and they will pick you up," I said to the flashlight man once the girls were safely in the helo.

Scott and I departed with a full aircraft for the Cloverleaf. The night sky was buzzing with helicopters and we could still see thousands of flashlights waving on all sides. As far as I could see, the scene was the same in every direction.

When we started this mission I had thought we might miss the action, showing up to find everyone rescued. As I looked out on the horizon I realized how wrong I was.

"Hang on, we're coming for you as fast as we can," was the thought I projected to those survivors not yet rescued. I only hoped we (meaning all the resources available to the U.S. Government) could get to everyone in time.

Eight hours after taking off we were required to return to the Coast Guard base and turn our aircraft over to a fresh crew, as we had flown as many hours as regulations allow and were required to rest. Halfway back to Mobile my adrenaline released its hold and I rested my chin on my chest. No dreams that night, only the black sleep of exhaustion. I woke with a nagging sense of guilt for having slept so well while others were still living a nightmare. I got ready to go again and headed down to the rescue swimmer shop in the main hangar, because I knew in a couple of hours a helicopter would return in search of a fresh crew.

AST2 Joel Sayers is one of a small number of rescue swimmers I helped train while I was assigned to Air Station in Elizabeth City, North Carolina. Short and powerfully built and intense, in many ways he reminds me of myself at a younger age. Having been a rescue swimmer since 1987, I feel a bond with anyone capable of completing the training. When I first meet Joel I doubted he could make it to the finish line. He had a chronic knee injury, and I was certain he couldn't overcome it. I later learned he used my doubts to spur him to show me how wrong I was. It hurt me when I learned he thought I considered him unworthy, when in truth I have never been more proud of anyone. I consider mental toughness the first requirement of a rescue swimmer.

In the days following Katrina, Joel led the way. He was one of the first swimmers on scene and was the one the news helicopter captured hacking a hole in the roof with an ax borrowed from a local fire-truck crew. He was improvising.

Just a couple of years before this hurricane, Joel and I had arranged and filmed a joint training exercise with the local fire department in Elizabeth City. Joel worked closely with the rescue crew to cut a "Patient" out of a wrecked car and transport her via helicopter. It was a learning experience for all, and the lessons learned help us understand the capabilities and challenges of working together. I hope it was one of the reasons Joel thought to ask the firefighters for an ax.

The next day, on 1 September Lcdr Jim O'Keefe was our aircraft commander, the same pilot from the day I consider the best duty day ever, and the executive officer (XO) from the Mobile base was the co-pilot. Our flight mechanic was AMT1 Herb Tisdale. Since Scott and I had flown together the previous day we were rested and ready to go at the same time again. Tasked to fly together, we knew from experience that made us faster. We headed out with an ax and the knowledge that there was still plenty of work left to do.

Just after lunch, before we boarded O'Keefe's helicopter, we had heard a news report of shots fired at rescue aircraft.

"Great," I thought with sarcasm, as I walked across the cement ramp.

We launched in mid-afternoon with a high searing sun overhead. Our first stop was a local ball field in the most devastated part of the Mississippi coast, to offload a pallet of drinking water and pick up a U.S. congressman for a tour of the area. My resentment at this delay was tempered by the hope that this person was evaluating needs so he could coordinate rescue assets. Otherwise he was endangering lives by wasting our time.

Scott and I hopped out onto the soft grass and saw three men dressed in jeans standing by the fence. A crowd gathered as our helicopter sat there with the rotor head turning, and I waved for several of the men to come closer as the XO, Herb, Scott, and I began to pass the water outward, hand to hand. These strangers would either help or have cases of drinking water slam into their chests when we tossed them. Only after we cleared the cabin and those first three men jumped in did I realize that I had put the congressman and his aides to work. They seemed glad to help. By the time we had completed this part of our mission and made our way back to the New Orleans rescue zone it was late afternoon.

O'Keefe is tall, lanky, sports a full mustache, and walks with a justified swagger. One of the best pilots in the Coast Guard, he had flown at maximum power (the red line) and at full speed, ignoring the violent shuddering, to get us back in the game.

Almost immediately Herb saw a white tee-shirt fluttering from a second floor window. O'Keefe swung the aircraft about and hovered off to the side of the house. A woman appeared and waved her arm.

"All right, Jerry and Scott, let's drop you guys down to that ledge in front of the window."

The double delivery method had now become so accepted by all the aircrews working the Katrina rescue zone that we didn't hesitate.

"Roger that sir, going off ICS," I said as Scott and I scooted to the door and connected to the hook Herb offered.

We noted a small section of first-floor roof that jutted out in front of a window, with water risen to the bottom of it leaving only the shingled part exposed. It was only a couple of feet wide and about five feet long, which made it a difficult target for Herb and O'Keefe to land us on. As we dangled on the hook, we swung back and forth a couple of times and started to spin, until I held out my arm and signaled Herb to pay out slack. When he did, Scott grabbed the edge of the second-floor eave to stop our swing, and Herb lowered us the rest of the way to the targeted roof. I went through the window first.

"Hi, my name is Jerry, are you two the only ones in the house?"

A woman said, "Yes. I don't know how you're going to get us out of here," and pointed at the man sitting on the bed. "He's paralyzed and can't walk."

I turned to Scott as he climbed through the window to ask, "Any ideas?"

The invalid was a very large man, and I hesitated to guess his weight in fear of offending him, but the look on my face must have suggested the challenge rolling around in my mind.

Scott and I looked at the window. After I walked down the second-floor hall to a balcony we had noticed on our approach, we talked to O'Keefe on the radio. We told him the window was too small, and the balcony was decorative and wouldn't hold any weight, so O'Keefe said, "Do whatever you gotta do."

"Send down the ax."

Herb lowered the ax to us in the basket and I grabbed it as Scott explained to our survivors that we would have to remove the window. I stepped back through, ax in hand, and tested the edges of the window frame by pushing on it. I didn't want to break the glass unless I had to, but as the metal edge of the window broke loose from the wood the glass shattered. We tossed all the shards out onto our landing spot, looked at our handiwork and then at our patient, back at each other and knew this was never going to work. He was too large. I poked my head through the window and evaluated the strength of the outside wall, then did the same with the inside wall and the window frame. After that I yanked the curtains off the wall and said, "Stand back."

Everyone backed up, and as I swung the ax with force, the bite of the blade cracked the wood frame. I let loose a series of swings and busted through the molding around the window and into the wall below it, then handed Scott the ax and told him to do the same to the other side. On his back swing, I kicked, and in less than two minutes we had destroyed the drywall, studs, insulation, wiring, and outside wall all the way to the floor. We had turned the window into a gaping, handicap-accessible exit the size of a sliding glass door.

I climbed out and cleared the glass and debris from our hoisting site, then signaled for the basket. As we waited for it to come down we lifted our patient, with much effort, into his chair and rolled him to the opening. I grabbed the basket and set it inside the bedroom on the floor. Scott and I grunted and heaved and, with our survivor helping as much as he was able, we got him in it.

We knew Herb couldn't to remove our patient from the basket, so Scott signaled for the sling, to be hoisted on his harness holding a folded wheelchair. I explained to our second survivor, the man's live-in nurse, that we would have to be hoisted together and that it was pretty scary.

Her answer, "No problem," made me smile.

"That was bravery," I thought.

Within a minute Herb had sent the sling down and I attached both of us. Just before we walked through the gaping hole to be hoisted I grabbed the ax, thinking, "We might need this later."

O'Keefe deftly landed in a very tight zone on the pavement at the Cloverleaf, where Herb hoisted our patient to the ground. We unloaded out two survivors quickly and wheeled one and walked the other to waiting emergency workers. I noticed far fewer ambulances and many more survivors than the last time I had been there.

"Stay with him," I told his nurse, before we left to continue the hunt.

All over the city people were still flooding the night sky with flash-lights and painting signs on their roofs. Another HH-60J hoisting patients from a hospital called over the radio for assistance. When the stories first surfaced about survivors shooting at helicopters, one rumor was that they came from a hospital. There were five hospitals in the flood zone, and I privately hoped that my fellow Coasties had not called for help because they had run into the person doing the shooting. O'Keefe calmly replied on the radio that we would be right there and tilted the airframe forward.

As we circled overhead, carefully losing altitude as we approached the hovering HH-60J that had hailed us, it departed to deliver their survivors. I looked down and saw people hugging the wall. The third floor of the hospital overlooked the offset roof, and almost every window along the wall had a face peering out of it. There was one body wrapped in a sheet, presumably dead, away from the rest of the crowd.

"Was this the gunman? Had they taken him out?" These were my thoughts as Scott and I descended to the deck below, not knowing what we might encounter. I remembered from my first tour in New Orleans that an afternoon thundershower could put two feet of water on the streets, and news stories predicted how many would die if the city ever took a direct hit from a hurricane of this magnitude. Having seen a great deal of death in my career, I have become somewhat philosophical about it. The way I heard it best described was in the movie *Braveheart*: "Everyone dies, but not everyone truly lives." If this turned out badly, I was comforted by the knowledge that I had lived hard.

I felt as if I just joined the Coast Guard a couple of years ago, not 40 years old. I felt 18 with 22 years of experience.

The Discovery Channel had sent a cameraman and producer to spend late spring and early summer of 2005 with us in search of good documentary footage, so our air station in Clearwater was not the only unit with a camera crew onboard. Several more were scattered around the country. In Clearwater, though, days and weeks passed between noteworthy SAR cases, and the camera crews had become frustrated.

"You guys should have waited until hurricane season," I told them one afternoon after another false flare sighting.

Being a Florida boy, hurricanes and I have a long and storied history together, including the busy 2004 season when four named storms slammed into my home state. The executives of the TV network extended their crew's time with us, then made the fateful decision to contract a second crew through the 2005 hurricane season. AST2 Jeremy Carroll had duty the night Katrina roared ashore and the cameras were rolling.

Jeremy was working the night shift in Clearwater so he could attend college during the day. He sports slicked-back hair and a bad-boy sneer that drives the ladies wild. Like almost any rescue swimmer Jeremy was ready for whatever he was to face.

With Lcdr Eric Gandee at the controls, he flew to Mobile during the early morning hours of Tuesday 30 August 2005. At first light Jeremy and his crew were in the flood zone hovering above a palatial home where three women waved from an open second floor window. The camera crew attached a small portable camera to his helmet and activated the portable recorder strapped to his back. (Earlier that summer AST1 Steve Garcia had designed and fabricated a pouch to hold the Discovery Channel's gear to a swimmer's back, with break-away straps should the bag become snagged.) He was hoisted down to the open window and climbed through. He talked to the ladies and learned that two of them were nurses who had been there since the levees broke, without food, water, or electricity.

"Is there anyway to get to the roof," he asked and they led him up to the attic but quickly discarded this idea when he couldn't break through. Back down at the window he looked out and considered going into the water, what we train for and where we feel comfortable.

"We made need to hoist from the window," he said to the crew hovering overhead on his radio. After discussing their options the aircrew lowered the hook to Jeremy, and he attached it to his harness. The flight mechanic then lowered him into the water, but he quickly learned there were too many hidden dangers for a water hoist when he slid off a car roof and cut open his leg. He raised and lowered his arm, touching the top of his head, the hand signal to go up. He leveled off at the window and explained to the ladies what was to come next. They hoisted the first one without difficulty. On the second evolution, though, the flight mechanic pulled Jeremy and his survivor away from the window before he had the sling completely wrapped around her, so Jeremy reached around her shoulders and held tight until they were inside the cabin.

Jeremy and his crew, some of the first rescuers in the flood zone, reported the extent of the devastation on their return to Mobile. Our leadership reacted to these reports by activating every asset at their disposal, including Coast Guard aircraft and cutters from all corners of the country, plus all available military helicopters.

This process began almost immediately, which was why I was

on the next logistical flight early Wednesday morning 31 August. That same night I was dangling from a hoist hook with Scott Rady, looking at a dead body on a roof, wondering if I was about to be shot and thinking of quotes from *Braveheart*.

My end was not to be that day, fortunately. Scott and I hit the deck and simultaneously raised our open palms to the sky. Jeremy Carroll was flying on his second sortie with the same crew, sans camera crew, and was already on the roof. We three exchanged greetings, hustled toward the expectant crowd, and formulated a plan.

We gathered near an open window with an army officer, facility maintenance manager, and an off-duty police officer. The army officer had been left by one of his unit's helicopter to triage patients. They were scheduled to return in about thirty minutes.

"All right, you make sure we keep families together and send us the worst ones first," Scott said to the officer, while I spoke with Jeremy about the hoist.

"Jeremy, you load them, Scott and I will bring them."

I turned to the maintenance man and asked him for a head count, noticing his bandaged foot for the first time.

"Two hundred."

"OK, just keep them calm and we'll get to work."

He nodded and limped to the window and climbed back through.

Jeremy pulled on his helmet and walked to a spot underneath the hovering helicopter, leaned against the blast of rotor wash, and signaled for a basket. Scott and I gathered on each side of the first patient and escorted her through the hurricane-force winds to the waiting basket and Jeremy. He had to set his body sideways and squatted down a foot to lower his center of gravity as he held the basket. We filled the aircraft with patients in wheelchairs, moms with infants, and family members until I lost count. Very familiar with the small cabin space of our helicopters, I wondered how the flight mechanic was able to fit in so many. Once the helicopter was full, the aircrew tilted the nose over and departed.

Jeremy's helicopter was hovering in line waiting for us to fill up the one departing and they moved overhead immediately, once it was clear. We didn't interrupt our ongoing operation, just kept bringing out patients and hoisting them.

The pilots called over the radio to report that the challenge of offloading the infirm at the Cloverleaf was overwhelming the emergency workers, so when we had filled Jeremy's aircraft he went with them to help and was hoisted holding a folding wheelchair.

With a minute to rest Scott and I removed our helmets and downed two bottles of water. Sweat had been pouring off both of us, and we needed to replenish ourselves.

The maintenance man asked, "Have you guys flown over Saint Bernard Parish?"

We had, and the news was not good. Part of the parish lies in the flight path to the Naval Air Station in Belle Chasse, Louisiana where we refueled our aircraft. The damage to this area was as severe as in much of the rest of New Orleans.

He confided in Scott and me, "I haven't spoken to anyone in my family since the storm. I don't know if they are alive."

"We could hoist you out and maybe you could find them. But you're injured," I said, pointing at his foot.

"Naw, I'm staying here until everyone is safe. I'll be the last man out."

In my career I have observed that the person that steps forward to assume leadership during a crisis is not always the most obvious one and may not have been the person in charge prior to the crisis. Because rescue swimmers usually work alone, I have traditionally relied on those natural leaders to help carry patients, control crowds, and make radio calls—do whatever was needed to accomplish the mission. I smiled, knowing I had found one here.

"My helicopter is inbound," the army officer said as he emerged from the hospital through the window. "Jerry, did you see that air-intake vent on the roof when that last sixty was hovering?" Scott asked. "It was bouncing up and looks like it is coming loose."

"You're right, I saw it too. Let's grab a couple of volunteers and throw that thing off the roof before that army bird shows up."

Scott, the police officer, the maintenance man, and I walked over to the aluminum air-intake vent and began to lift. It was 12 feet by 12 feet across and about 3 feet high, not too heavy for the four of us to tear loose. Had we not scuttled it, it might have flown free and brought down a helicopter. But as we flipped it over the edge of the roof into the water I failed to jump back quickly enough, so that the metal edge gouged my shin and knee, not enough to leave a cool scar, just enough to embarrass me. "Damn it," I thought as I stared at the skin ripped from my shin, from the top of my boot to my knee.

I knew from experience the Huey lacked hoist capability and wondered if the roof would even hold the aircraft. Scott and I looked at the landing zone dotted with pipe and vents and ducts. Another helicopter, possibly the one the officer had arrived on, had landed and sunk into the asphalt leaving indentations six inches deep.

"I hope like hell that helo doesn't fall through the roof." I was thinking.

When the distinctive chop of a Huey alerted us to its arrival, we turned to the army officer, who had identified a heart patient too scared and possibly too injured to survive a hoist and had brought him to the roof. We agreed that the patient and his family would go, as well as three other patients unable to get out of bed. As this medivac Huey had a rack capable of holding three litter-bound patients, quickly, and with the help of our group, we identified the three women who needed to go.

The remaining hospital workers and other survivors inside the hospital wheeled our next three patients to the window. Scott brought the folded litters off the helicopter, and one by one we unfolded and locked them open and placed our patients on them. These litters are fabricated from green cotton duck with wood handles that run their length. This design has been around since before World War II, and I just hoped these litters were not that old. They lacked straps to secure patients, and once inside the aircraft had to be lifted to the metal locking hooks bolted to the deck and ceiling. We carried the lightest patient first and lifted her to the top set of hooks, repeating the process until all three slots were filled. Scott and I backed away as the army officer gave a wave and boarded the aircraft.

In the moment of quiet after the Huey departed, the maintenance man asked me, "What do you want to do with the dead bodies? We have a lot more inside."

I turned subconsciously toward the body under the sheet. "Nothing for now. Let's worry about the living, there'll be time enough later to bury the dead." I didn't ask how many or causes of deaths, matters that seemed less important than making sure no more were added to their number.

Scott and I donned our helmets as we heard the next helicopter; it was time to get back to work. The door of the aircraft slid open and Jeremy's legs popped out. He was hoisted to the deck, and after he held his palm upward, came hustling over to me.

"The pilots are heavy with a full tank of gas and want the smallest survivors, two at a time," he yelled in my ear. As I turned around and looked at the survivors lined up against the wall I knew we couldn't honor their request. I just nodded my head and told Jeremy to get ready, that Scott and I would bring them to him.

We brought forward the patients we had triaged and believed needed to go next. Jeremy knew what I was doing and nodded, in agreement as I pushed the first wheelchair-bound woman out. With each patient, I factored the hoisting of relatives and adjusted my next choice to make sure families stayed together. The process was time-consuming as we added additional hoists to load wheelchairs, for without the chairs we couldn't unload our patients at the other end.

When the flight mechanic looked down and gave Jeremy the slash-throat signal, he meant they had all they could hold. Jeremy was hoisted up, turned around in the open door, and gave a little wave of support as the aircraft steadily climbed.

Scott and I loaded two more helicopters full of survivors during the next hour. As our aircraft moved back in over our heads I turned to look at the remaining survivors and was shocked to see two more ladies in wheelchairs against the wall. We had already evaluated the sick and injured and hoisted all the wheelchair patients. "Where had these come from?" I thought. One held what looked like a baby. When I left Scott and ran over to the woman, I saw that she had swaddled her dog to look like a baby and was cradling it like one.

"Look," I told her. "I've got no problem taking dogs. I got two yesterday, but people come first. You'll have to wait until last to go." She nodded, and when I turned to look inside the window, I saw five more survivors with their dogs. I shook my head and turned to the maintenance man. "Keep the people with dogs here until last."

I then moved back to the front of the line where I grabbed the next man in line. "Are you ready?" The process began again. Scott held the basket on the ground as I ran toward him with the survivor. The patient objected, mildly. "I just had a heart attack and bypass surgery last week. Can you slow down?"

"You bet," I said, wishing I had known so I could have used a wheelchair.

O'Keefe interrupted my thoughts with a radio call as I walked back toward the line, his voice blaring from the mike strapped to my harness riser on my right shoulder. "Bring the lady with the baby next."

When I explained the circumstances around our new "Mom" he agreed we should continue as planned. I brought the next patient in line to Scott.

When this aircraft was full the flight mechanic pointed at Scott and me and waved his hand to come to him. We knew this meant we were to go with the aircraft, and a quick glance at my watch confirmed we had been on this sortie for close to seven hours. We had worked the hospital roof for almost six of those and it was time to go. I ran back to the maintenance man, whose name I never got, shook his hand, and said, "Nice job. We've got to go now, but keep waving the flashlights at the helicopters. They will come and pick you up. And I'll let them know you guys are waiting for rescue. Before I leave, tell me how many are left?"

"Thirty," he said with a smile.

In six hours, with a lot of help, we had rescued 170 people and never met the first gunman.

Scott and I connected our harnesses and were whisked up. It was 1 AM when O'Keefe turned the helicopter back toward Mobile.

Between flights into the "Rescue Zone," our mandatory crew-rest requirement was satisfied by sleeping in any empty bed in the overflowing barracks, RVs in the parking lot, or on the floor of the swimmer shop. We practiced hot racking, with one swimmer using the bed of another who was flying. As soon as we had satisfied the requirement, 10 hours of time off, we returned to the swimmer shop to await the next aircraft.

By the third day Scott and I were with about ten other swimmers lounging on the stiff military couches, waiting. Restlessness was our constant companion, and we looked for ways to help with the effort or pass the time. We checked and rechecked our EMT gear, we held chainsaw use lessons for the inexperienced, and we ate. Several local restaurants had heard what was happening and donated every type of food imaginable.

It was on this day that Master Chief Scott Dyer, the man in charge of the swimmer program, came charging through the door. Chief Dave Moore had been on his feet for almost 24 hours and was leaning over a grease board trying to make sense of chaos. Moore explained to Dyer that the board depicted which swimmers were flying, who was inbound, who was sleeping, and who was waiting to go. Dyer's organized mind quickly identified our needs, and he began to use his considerable influence to satisfy them.

In a few hours and after a handful of calls, Dyer had more swimmers on their way, axes stacked in the corner, a Critical Incident Stress Debriefing Team on station, and several more non-flying supervisors available to help Moore.

It was also on this day, back in Clearwater, that AST1 Steve Garcia arranged with our unit supply team and our engineering officer, Cdr. Anthony Vogt, to supply us with sleeping bags, inflatable mattresses, knee pads (for those roofs), and cases of Red Bull. Steve had those items and other relief materials on a pallet and shipped via a contracted commercial fixed-wing aircraft within 12 hours of my call.

Before this was over, more than 60 of the 311 rescue swimmers in the Coast Guard would fly missions over New Orleans. Many of those swimmers were already swapping stories with each other and with the steady stream of reporters beginning to show up.

AST1 Scott Holloway, a burly New Englander, who was the first to use a chainsaw to rip open a roof, saving four people, shared his story with a heavy Massachusetts accent. The only "little sister" rescue swimmer we had had flying, AST2 Sara Faulkner, was almost mobbed by a desperate crowd. After his helicopter hoisted him down then departed with a mechanical problem AST2 Tim Wamble, a tall lean swimmer from Elizabeth City, wandered the flooded streets of the Ninth Ward looking for survivors. To get to a group of survivors in an apartment building, AST2 Emerson waded through floating feces. There were stories on every side.

The most disturbing one I heard was at second hand, so the details were few. A Navy helicopter was hoisting survivors with a sling, which is usually reserved for military persons, unless used in conjunction with a rescue swimmer. The danger with the sling is that a survivor who raises his arms above his head can unknowingly fall, and this movement is a common reaction as one approaches the bottom of an aircraft during a hoist. I was told that such a thing happened to a woman who fell from the door of a helicopter to her death, her husband and children watching in horror as she slammed into the roof in front of them. The Navy aircrew immediately called for assistance, and a Coast Guard aircraft swooped in and lowered AST3 Moses "Mo" Rivera down. Mo knew it was too late. The Navy aircraft departed scene and left Mo and his crew to finish the grisly task.

As a rule, we rescue survivors before recovering the dead, and this remained our practice throughout this operation. Every rescue swimmer had been leaving the bodies behind, just as Scott and I had done in the hospital. However, Mo thought the trauma of leaving this woman's body while the rest of the family was recovered would be too much for them to bear, so he hoisted them all.

As I listened to these stories and others, I realized I was part of an unprecedented rescue operation, the likes of which none of us had ever seen.

"Jerry, you're up next," Moore said, shocking me from my thoughts.

Lcdr Conley was again my aircraft commander and broke the bad news: "Today's mission is for us to fly to Lake Front Airport in New Orleans and fix and recover the six zero four two." An aircrew from the night before had made a precautionary landing when a warning light illuminated.

The hurricane had virtually destroyed the airport's main structures, and countless small private planes were piled high like discarded toys. But the runways were clear, and many of the aircraft working the zone had used them. The 6042 sat on one of them.

I am not an aircraft mechanic, but I was assigned in case the aircraft could be repaired and released to continue rescue operations. After two hours on deck, our maintenance crew had repaired the problem, and we strapped in for another day of work.

Smoke billowed up from several fires, and a quarter-mile of industrial dock front was engulfed in flames. With the radio chatter steady, and as soon as the wheels left the ground Conley was fishing for business. By this time a fixed-wing aircraft was providing a semblance of air traffic control and an operational control, center was assigning missions.

Instead of a mission we heard, "Attention all aircraft, shots have been fired from the Memorial Hospital. All aircraft are order to stay clear of the hospital by three miles." Conley called and advised them the 6042 was a Coast Guard hoist-capable HH-60J, with a rescue swimmer on board.

The orders came back straightaway: "We have a report of six severely sick patients at Algiers Point Ferry Terminal, proceed immediately."

Conley did one low pass to evaluate the landing zone, then an approach to a gravel parking lot that was barely larger than our rotor span. After he set the aircraft down gently in the cloud of the dust, I jumped out. Coasties with two day's growth of beard greeted me with shocked relief. I didn't know to which unit they belonged but guessed from their appearance they had been there for a while.

"Bring the medivac patients," I yelled to the first man I approached. They had made the request some time ago, and when an aircraft did not immediately respond, moved the patients out of the sun and back into the ferry terminal. I followed them up the dike to the main building, to find at least 200 people, all with the look of war-weary refugees, in and around the terminal.

All six patients were diabetics who had been without their medication for days. The complications from this disease could be devastating, including loss of limbs, even death, if not treated daily. We quickly found 5 of the 6 patients and began carrying them on litters and stretchers back down the hill. The 6th was missing.

One of my patients refused to leave if her 16-year-old daughter could not go with her, even if it meant she might die.

"Bring the daughter," I shouted over the rotor noise.

When I ran back toward my fellow Coasties to learn if our last patient had been found one of them asked if I could arrange helicopter transport for the rest of the stranded survivors. The shock of the request made me hesitate for a second.

"I'll see what I can do."

As it turned out, I could do very little. I called Conley on the radio and passed on the request, which he passed to the operation center. When it became obvious that the last patient was not to be found, I boarded the helicopter and closed the door.

Conley had more luck than I, because as soon as he added power and tilted the aircraft forward, a Navy CH-53, Sea Stallion was making an approach to the landing spot we had vacated. This aircraft can haul up to 50 survivors.

The Cloverleaf was no longer the drop-off point for survivors, as the sheer quantity of them had overwhelmed rescue workers. The new spot was New Orleans International Airport and we headed west to make our drop.

One of the involved pilots described the flying as being in the Wild West. There were so many aircraft in the skies over New Orleans, I was amazed no one had a midair collision. Flying was a constant near-miss for all aircrews; the closest I have ever experienced to slamming into other aircraft was at New Orleans International Airport.

A dozen helicopters were making approaches into semi-controlled airspace (the tower was making advisories), avoiding each other by sheer pilot diligence and luck. We lined up 20 aircraft in two parallel lines to offload survivors. FEMA had organized fire departments, ambulance crews, soldiers, airport employees, and volunteers into ground workers. Those able to walk were loaded onto baggage carts and transported to the terminal to board outbound flights. For the sick or injured I jumped out onto the tarmac and held up fingers equal to the number of patients, so the ground crew brought out that many foldable green litters. The patients were then driven to waiting ambulances or to the triage center inside. While the ground crews were very efficient, the multiple launches of numerous helicopters straight up and forward really bothered me. The rotor wash blasted everyone and the other aircraft as the helicopters flew straight toward the tower, circling it to either side. To me this was pure madness; someone was going to die.

We departed the airport, narrowly missing a Navy HH-60J circling the other side of the tower, and headed back to Mobile. The helicopter required more maintenance, and we were close to our maximum allowable flight hours.

After we landed I hauled my tired self to the swimmer shop, with my ax handle poking prominently out of from my swimmer bag. That had been the first sortie on which I hadn't had to use my ax to complete at least one rescue, and I felt dejected. My ax had taken on a life of its own, and I had dubbed it "The Redecorator", even painting the name on the handle.

Senior Chief Brad Torrens told me, "Jerry, be here at 0730 hours tomorrow, you're going to meet the President."

"Yeah, right," I said.

Torrens, coordinating the swimmers during the overnight hours, smiled as he said it. I did not believe him.

"I'm serious," he responded.

As I would soon discover, meeting the President was not beyond belief at all, because AST3 Josh Mitcheltree, another swimmer working in the Katrina rescue zone, had received a call from the President on his cell phone the day before.

"Damn, I get to meet the President," I thought as I piled in an empty rack back in the barracks later that night.

The flight surgeon had been by the swimmer shop many times during the last several days, making sure we took in enough fluids, preloading our intestinal tracts by dosing us with Pepto-Bismol tablets, and stitching cuts. He also instructed us to not shave while we were being exposed to the toxic water in New Orleans. So far I had been subjected to spray from the rotor wash, but hadn't entered the water. Nevertheless, with this thought in mind the next morning I shaved in order to look presentable just in case.

"What do you mean, he hasn't left D.C. yet?" I asked at 10 AM the next morning as Chief Warrant Officer Ken Hardenbrook passed the word among the crews. I could have slept in.

I had never met him before, though after hurricane Isabel in 2003 he stopped by Air Station Elizabeth City. At that time the executive officer, Cdr. Jim Sherman—an excellent officer, man and pilot—was selected to greet him as he descended the steps of his jet. He carefully considered what to say to the President, given the once-in-a-lifetime chance.

"Let's take the space program to Mars, Mr. President," he said, revealing his secret desire to see mankind conquer this challenge. I thought his comment was a good one, but the President's comeback was better.

"That's a fine idea, but we've gotta kick a little Al Qaeda ass first."

After 9-11 I was very angry and, for the first time, wished I had joined another service—one where I could have been the hammer this nation swung in response. When Sherman shared this insight with the rest of the crew I knew I had found My President.

Secret Service agents soon closed the hangar doors, set up a perimeter, and began checking IDs of everyone in the area. Shortly before Air Force One set down, all those who had been invited to stand in line and shake the President's hand were mustered on the hangar deck. The Aviation Training Center's command master chief instructed all of us to look busy in the background, as we were to be props for a presidential sound bite. He then looked at the four swimmers standing among the 50 Coasties and asked which one wanted to be in swimmer gear.

We huddled together and decided. "If one us is required then we all will," I said.

We were ready and waiting when the President walked to the podium and praised the work of the rescuers, then turned to the FEMA director and uttered those now infamous words, "You're doing a good job, Brownie."

In person, now, he seemed more like a man than a larger-than-life figure. I watched him as he made his way down the line shaking hands. I too was contemplating what to say, now that my chance was coming.

As he worked down the line, I considered asking him to sign "The Redecorator". An hour earlier I had brought this idea up to the Secret Service Agent who was briefing us on acceptable behavior around the President, stuff like, do not make any sudden moves, physically assault him, and such. He laughed and said even he would be thrown to the ground if he carried an ax out for the President to sign. "No axes around Dubya—Got it." I thought.

Just then AST1 Tim Fortney, an elder swimmer like me who had graduated from swimmer school two weeks before I did, came running up and handed me a rescue swimmer coin. "Hand this to the man," he said. I pictured my face planted in the cement with a boot on my neck and passed the coin to the young swimmer standing next to me. "Here, hand this to the man," I said with a wry grin.

Then he gets to me. "It's an honor to meet you, Mr. President," I said, as he took my hand.

He stopped and lingered for a minute. "Not everyone has a chance to make a difference in other people's lives. You guys are making a difference. Keep up the good work."

"Thank you, Mr. President. We will."

He moved on down the line, occasionally sharing similar thoughts with others. When he was done he walked over to the crowd gathered at the podium. "Is Josh Mitcheltree here? I would like to meet him."

I have never witnessed so much scrambling as that request provoked. Within seconds Fortney had rushed Josh from the swimmer shop. The glad-handing and smiles lasted but a few seconds and President Bush was gone, whisked by his schedule-keepers back to Air Force One.

As I walked back to the swimmer shop I contemplated our forty-third president and concluded that he is a good man. When a man, any man, is stripped of all those things others use to define him, such as social status and material possessions, the essence of his being is his ability to keep his word. I harbor no doubts that George W. Bush's word is ironclad and worthy of my respect.

I waltzed though the door of the swimmer shop and asked Moore to put me back in the lineup, ready to go again.

I did not fly again until first light on Sunday morning 4 September. Lt. David Schell, a Clearwater pilot I have flown with many times, was my aircraft commander, with Ltjg. Adam Spencer in the copilot seat. Schell has a dry wit that makes flying with him fun. In the back with me was AST1 Dustin Skarra, a swimmer I had known for years who had just transferred to Mobile from the Coast Guard's EMT school in Petaluma, California.

On the ground at Air Station New Orleans many of the crew had suffered catastrophic destruction of their homes and hangar yet, they had been maintaining aircraft and flying around the clock. Their families were hundreds of miles away, jobless and homeless. They were working to help others stay alive and start over while putting their own needs on hold. Someone in the Coast Guard chain of command recognized this and funneled other Coasties in to stand their duty, giving them a much-needed break. Our first stop of the day was to the tarmac of the air station, where we delivered two more enlisted Coasties.

As soon as the rotor brake was applied a man came jogging up to Schell's door, several cameras dangling from his neck. "I'm a staff photographer with Reuters. You guys mind if I tag along?"

We were fueled and airborne in few minutes. It was Day Six after the levees broke, and the concern about survivors had me flying with a sense of urgency. The heat was brutal, the water filled with gas, oil, and sewage. Leaking gas lines had caused numerous buildings to burn to the water, with more waiting for a spark. Yet with people dying just because they were still there, I encountered the first victims who did not want to leave.

We flew low tight circles over the French Quarter and saw several people wading in the streets. Most waved us off, refusing to be hoisted. We bounded over a power line when Schell saw a young man motioning us to come here to him. The water was about waist deep and level with the first floor of the house. Several kids wandered into the street as the earth-shaking noise of the helicopter pounded their roof. In an instant I was attached to the hook and on my way down, ax in hand.

So far I had not entered the water at all, though I had been routinely sprayed by rotor wash. With the dire warnings of our flight surgeon ringing in my head I had no intention of ever entering the water and had opted to wear my flight suit for this sortie.

I landed on the roof and yelled to the kids below. They told me their mom could not walk, and they refused to leave without her. I wandered over the roof looking for a way into the house hoping I could bring them to the roof, but it was solid and tight.

"Damn it," I thought, knowing I needed to get into the water and go through the door.

The roof was at least 12 feet off the ground, surrounded by blackish-brown sludge and reeking of something like sewage but worse. I jumped, arms spread wide to the roof of a car parked in the back drive, and vaulted over a wood fence before I could change my mind. I grimaced as I landed with a splash on the sidewalk. "Great! Just great! What a smell I have discovered," I said out loud to no one. I sloshed around the building to be greeted by the toothy grins of five little kids.

The aircrew had followed my progress and hover-taxied back to keep me where they could see me. I seemed to have my own personal hurricane following me wherever I went. The wind was whipping everything in out and up, loose debris pelting us all. I spoke to the kids in a calm but loud voice, ignoring the helicopter, as if this sort of thing happened every day.

Mom had been carried to the front door, and I explained what to expect as they were hoisted. I then called the aircrew on the radio, and we agreed that the best hoisting site was a raised median dividing the street. Schell, concerned about clearance from the power lines, told me this was to be a high hoist, so I requested Dustin be sent down to help. As I waited for him the streets came alive with people.

Faces appeared in several windows, a young kid ran up to me and pointed and yelled although I couldn't hear him, and an older man in white shorts and no shirt waded up and gave me an envelope.

"Are you ready to go?" I asked him curious about the paper in my hand.

"No, no, I just wanted to volunteer my services," he said pointing at his chest. "Ex-Marine."

"Come on and go with me," I said, then repeated to him what I had been told about the toxicity of the water.

"Its OK," he said. "My wife and I will be fine."

I turned back to the young man, who had beckoned to us just as Dustin gave me a hand signal that he was ready for my first survivor. He was a little older than the kids I was about to put in the basket, and I asked for his help keeping them together and calm.

"Here, hold my ax while I put your mom in the basket," I told the oldest sibling. They watched, fascinated, as I squatted down and lifted their mother onto my back. Hiking through the water was treacherous, and I found debris and the curb the hard way, almost stumbling. Dustin knelt next to the basket and helped me load our survivor, keeping her on the ground while I hustled back for the two smallest children.

I picked up a toddler and told her to wrap her arms around my neck, then asked the young man who had come running up to help me escort another little boy out to their mother. He and I put our arms under the boy, leaned forward against the wind, and splashed our way back to Dustin. Dustin, the neighborhood boy, and I hoisted the entire family, then several more people who had made their way down the street.

"How about you?" I asked when we were done.

"I can't leave my mom."

I again explained the probability of death and hoped he would change his mind. He was not swayed, but told me of another elderly lady on his block who would not survive much longer and volunteered to show me to her house.

A loose section of tin roof was swaying from a power line in front of a small green house about half a block south. We slogged our way down the street around the tin and carried the lady out on our shoulders. She clung to our torsos and bravely faced the wind, though it was stinging us with needles of spray.

Several other people came out onto the street, some just to watch, others to look for lost loved ones. One showed me a picture of his father. I told them another aircraft or rescue craft would be along to pick them up, because they needed to leave if they wanted to live. Before I was hoisted I convinced the young man to get his mother out of New Orleans the first chance he had and he promised he would. I waved to him as I swung from the hoist cable, ax in hand.

Schell dropped our survivors at the airport and made top speed back to the same block, to find an amphibious boat/truck driving the street and picking up those we had left behind. I never did see the young man again and regretted not having a chance to tell him how proud I was of his bravery. I still believe that real leadership is earned and turns up in the least expected places.

With time, the rescues were fewer and we had to hunt for our next survivors. We had found many more people in houses, on balconies, wading through water, but none of them wanted rescue.

"Look at the dead body on top of the van," the flight mechanic called out on the ICS.

None of us was sure this was a dead body, so Schell swung around and pulled into a hover for a closer look over a blue van submerged up to its roof. On top was a body wrapped in a white sheet, not moving.

"Sure looks dead," I said.

Then he moved. The sheet whipped open, and a man leaned up on one elbow.

"No, he's alive," Schell said. "What about a direct deployment?"

The van was under two oak tree canopies and directly under a set of power lines, a tight spot that did not allow for a low-hoist altitude. The maneuver would be very dangerous to me, should I become entangled. "Let's do it," I said, as I slid to the open door and readied myself.

Schell and the flight mechanic worked to thread me through the slim opening between the tree limbs and under the power lines. My legs dipped into the water, and I leaned back to grab the rail on top of the van as I swung past, pulled myself out of the water, and sat next to my survivor. He watched my mouth move but seemed unable to speak himself. He looked dazed and emaciated, making me wonder how long he had been up there. Although I was never sure he knew what I was telling him, I explained what I was about to do and slipped the sling over his shoulders and under his arms. His face froze in a mask of sheer terror when we were lifted together from the van's roof. I kept the power lines in my peripheral, ready to fend off should the need arise, but hoped to avoid finding out if they were still alive. The Reuters photographer snapped some very good shots of the two of us coming up, and Dustin filmed the whole rescue as he looked over the flight mechanic's shoulder. It was over in less than three minutes.

We still had room to hoist more survivors but elected to drop our lone survivor off at the triage center and refuel. While on the ground I changed back into my wet suit and stuffed my soaked flight suit and boots into my gear bag.

Dustin and I worked several more roofs, and I busted open one more window with "The Redecorator". We landed in a ball field and loaded several more who had held out hoping for the water to go down. Lowered to a roof, Dustin met a man who refused to leave even as a dead body floated nearby. At the end of our 6 hour mission we dropped the photographer back at New Orleans, fueled up, and turned to the east for Mobile.

This was my last foray into the rescue zone over New Orleans. I was rotated out, back to my home station of Clearwater the next day. I had lost count of the number of persons I had rescued and arriving at a tally was difficult because we worked in teams and with multiple aircraft. Before all was said and done more than a quarter of the 311 Coast Guard rescue swimmers would participate in rescues over the city, in the largest search and rescue effort in recorded history. The Coast Guard gathered enough information in post-action reports to conclude that Coasties had rescued 33,500 survivors.

CHAPTER 15

The Hatch

On my first duty night back in Clearwater after the Katrina rescues I was awakened from a deep sleep by the piercing sound of the SAR alarm.

"Put the ready H-sixty on the line, boat taking on water."

I ran from the air-conditioned building onto the tarmac and threw my gear bag in the back of the helicopter. My pilot was a jaunty exchange officer from the United Kingdom, Lt. Anthony Gear, who told us in his British accent that a cell phone call had come in from one of the men on the boat as it was going down.

It was almost midnight, the humidity so oppressive it was difficult to breathe as we climbed into the airframe. During the flight we buzzed several boats before finding the one we were looking for. A foot or two of the bow was pointed toward the sky, and three men clung to it and each other. Gear eased the helo into a hover, careful to keep the frightened fishermen outside the blast of rotor wash. Within a minute I was swimming through the warm waters of the Gulf of Mexico.

"Hey, are the fish biting?" I asked as I reached them, then stopped the next joke in my throat as I saw their silver dollar-sized-eyes staring at me in disbelief. The small fiberglass boat was leaking fuel into the water, and one of them was gagging on it. Everything was covered in gasoline and they were all trying to keep as much of their bodies out of the water as possible, even climbing on another's shoulders when they could.

Five minutes and four hoists later, we were inside the aircraft, gasoline fumes burning all our noses. We were covered in fuel. A

166

heavyset young man leaned forward to look outside, never having flown in a helicopter. Many survivors have done the same through the years, and I slid back to give him a better view.

"Man, we were scared to death…I'm going to kill that guy that worked on my boat…we were pissed when we saw you guys fly right by us." His sentences all ran together. "We were in a three-day shark-fishing tournament… man, we had chum in the water."

"You were lucky," I thought and smiled.

I asked them to donate one of their lifejackets to our collection of many from our rescues, which we hang high on the wall. They agreed and signed their names to it as well.

Normally a sea story like this would be worth sharing, but in the wake of Katrina such an episode paled. This time I didn't rescue 50 people or hack open a roof with my ax. I'm glad Katrina happened at the end of my career rather than at the start of it, so I didn't spend 20 years comparing it to all other rescues.

The end of my career, that phrase marked a drastic life change. I officially hung up my fins on 1 May 2006 and left the Coast Guard with high hopes for rescue swimmers. Occasionally, as I approached my final days in Coast Guard blue, I was asked what I would miss, and my answer might have sounded strange: "Christmas cards."

It is an annual tradition for rescue-swimmer shops to take a photo of all the assigned swimmers, create a Christmas card, and mail it to all the other shops. We looked forward to them eagerly every year and posted them on the bulletin board near the front door.

As with all things swimmers do this became a competition. In the 1990s each shop tried to trump all the others. We had computer-generated free falls from the Empire State Building and from inside the Patriots' home stadium, amusement park mermaids, and of course the #2 card of all time, the cast of "Baywatch." The Los Angeles swimmers posed with the cast of that show, and their card would have been #1 if we Clearwater swimmers hadn't gone them one better.

This happened during my first tour in Clearwater, and I remember how we mumbled and grumbled about wanting to top this card. We drove to the beach, ate hot wings at Hooters, snapped pictures of us with girls in bikinis and short shorts, but none of these pictures came close to being number one. As the beer kicked in and our judgement faded, we ended up at the local adult dance establishment, a place we refer to as the Ballet, where we shot film of swimmers wearing wetsuits up on stage, wrapped around the pole, with dancers waving dollars as they looked up.

When the smoke cleared and we had mailed the apology letter, we retired #1, warned by our CO to not try and top this card.

In other words being a rescue swimmer is like belonging to a fraternity—I will miss my brothers.

They still have many miles to go before they finish becoming. While sitting in the shop in Mobile during Katrina, I remember watching Dyer huddle over the grease board with Moore and sigh as he ran his palm over his cropped hair.

"We need more swimmers," he told Moore as they looked at the board trying to assign a swimmer or two to every helicopter going to New Orleans. We did our jobs well during the days and weeks following Katrina. How many more could we have saved had there been more of us?

The creation of the rescue swimmer program was a painful transition resisted by many but forced upon us by an insightful Congress. Since bringing it online in 1984 the Coast Guard has made many improvements of its own accord. There was a time, at the beginning of my career, when the announcement following the SAR alarm didn't always included the aircraft commander's request for a swimmer, many times they did not. Since that time we have proven ourselves so indispensable that aircraft commanders' would never think of flying farther than a couple of miles from home plate without one. The Coast Guard did not create enough rescue swimmer billets to satisfy current demand. Those who formulate the current search and rescue strategies must also create more rescue swimmer billets in order for us to achieve the assigned missions.

One hot summer evening, 120 miles off the coast of North Carolina I was hoisted to a boat where the crew was performing CPR on a man. I used every skill I had been trained to use as an EMT basic, yet the man still died. I do not know if he would have made it had I been trained to a higher level, but I went to sleep that night wishing I had been able to find out.

Civilian air ambulance services require --at minimum-- a paramedic or nurse to provide patient care. Our Eleventh District commanders require rescue swimmers to train to the next higher level, because they have learned that we can save more lives. I hope and predict that in the near future the Coast Guard will mandate a greater level of medical training for all rescue swimmers.

During the late 1990s, three fishermen in an overturned boat off the coast of Cape Cod had tried to claw their way out of the air pocket in which they were trapped. The Coast Guard responded, but no Coasties were then trained as divers. Our crews called the local dive team and flew them to the boat, but not in time.

Dive rescue is not a skill we frequently require, but having it could save lives. With our current training focused on open-water surface rescues, this skill is an obvious next step that is long overdue.

I, like most men, have been called many names during the course of a career. One of my favorites was "Rescue Jerry." The pilot that gave it to me wanted me to be made into a GI Joe action figure. "Damn good idea," I thought. The one other swimmers will remember me by, is "The Creeker." For if one lives in the backwoods of Florida as I do, eventually the floor will creak under his weight, and when it does they are a Creeker. But the one that brings back the strongest memories was, "Mr. Flaresighting."

For a time while I was stationed in Elizabeth City I had too many flare-sighting SAR cases to count. I hate this type of case, often reported by well-meaning but grossly misinformed civilians we call Condo Commandos. They sit on the balconies and report red flashing lights of airplanes, fireworks, shooting stars, flashlights, and many imagined sightings as flare sightings. To attempt to dissuade them is to question their veracity and integrity. Most of the time there are no corroborating reports despite many others who might support the claim.

We could save millions of dollars by requiring removal of all shooting pyrotechnic flares from all boats. Flares were originally used to alert life saving stations along the coast as a ship went down. Now, with the advances in communication, they merely waste time and money. Yes, those who have been rescued using flares might argue otherwise, but they need to be brought into the present, kicking and screaming if necessary.

As I am shown the hatch, though, I have no worries about the future. At my last EMT recertification class in Petaluma, California, I sat next to Scott Dyer, now Master Chief Dyer, and the Rescue

Swimmer Program Manager. We talked about what the future holds and that all the changes I envisioned—advanced EMT skills, dive rescue, parachute rescue—are still being talked about at the highest levels. I believe this is where rescue swimmers are headed. The Coast Guard will succeed, and what it means to be a Coast Guard rescue swimmer will continue to evolve.

The milestone swimmers had celebrated on 23 January 2001 for surpassing the mark of four thousand lives saved seems meaningless now when compared to how many lives we saved in the wake of Katrina. We knocked that earlier number from the ring during two hectic weeks in September of 2005.

But Katrina's most remarkable effect was the one it had on me. Katrina was the test that conquered my fear, yet not in the way I expected. I had hoped for one great physical battle against the forces of nature, man against wind and waves. Instead, Katrina tested the mettle of a nation, the resolve of millions, and our value of life over infighting. Some failed, some were valiant. The Coast Guard possessed a will of iron, the resolve of Titans. I was but a small part of our overall effort.

But for me day after day of physical exertion, of nonstop flying, energy-sapping adrenaline letdown, all tested my concept of what it meant to be challenged. This wasn't the ending I had hoped for, it was far greater. The weight upon my shoulders was gone and had learned that the only way to fail is to stop trying. My mettle had been tested. I had been challenged, and I did not hesitate or quit. As I returned to the ordinary world, I would not fail. I still had so much I wanted to do in this life. I had another log cabin to build on my new timber farm in Tennessee, outdoor adventures to chase, stories to tell.

I would start by writing about my time as a rescue swimmer. I would call it *Brotherhood of the Fin*.

Glossary of Abbreviations

AST Aviation Survival Technician, the enlisted rating that has the helicopter rescue swimmer collateral duty.

ASM Aviation Survivalman, the name of the enlisted rating from 1965 to 1998. changed to AST in the rate merger of 1998

AD Aviation Machinist Mate, aircraft engine and power plant maintenance rating.

AM Aviation Structural Mechanic, aircraft airframe mechanic.

AMT Aviation Maintenance Technician, is the combination of AD and AM, in the rate merger of 1998

AE Aviation Electricians Mate, aircraft wiring and electrical systems mechanic.

AT Aviation Electronics Technician, aircraft avionics mechanic.

AVT Aviation Avionics Technician, is the combination of AE and AT in the rate merger of 1998.

DC Damage Controlman, shipboard emergency repair and response specialist.

E-1 thru E-10 Uniform enlisted pay scale used by all five military branches.

O-1 thru O-10 Uniform Officer pay scale.

Non-rate E-1 thru E-3, enlisted person not yet trained in a job specialty.

Airman E-3, enlisted person learning basic aviation practices and awaiting job specialty training.

Petty Officer All E-4 through E-6 are enlisted non-commissioned officers. E-4 is a third class petty officer, E-5 is a second class petty officer, and E-6 is a first class petty officer.

Chief Petty Officer E-7 enlisted non-commissioned officer, addressed as "Chief."

Senior Chief Petty Officer E-8 enlisted non-commissioned officer, addressed as "Senior Chief."

Master Chief Petty Officer E-9 enlisted non-commissioned officer, addressed as "Master Chief."

Note: When written, all non-commissioned officers are identified by rate then rank, for example, an AST1 holds a paygrade of E-6 and is addressed as Petty Officer last name.

Lt Lieutenant, paygrade O-3, commissioned officer.

Lcdr Lieutenant Commander, O-4, commissioned officer.

Cdr Commander, O-5, senior commissioned officer.

Capt Captain, O-6, senior commissioned officer. Also, the commanding officer of any unit is referred to as Captain regardless of rank held.

EMT Emergency Medical Technician

ICS Internal Communication System, inside an aircraft.

SAR Search and Rescue

MAST Military Anti Shock Trousers.

XO Executive Officer

CO Commanding Officer

Fm flight mechanic

Rs rescue swimmer

PIC pilot in command

AC Aircraft Commander

Creeker A creeker is any person that has spent a lifetime in mobile home, back woods hunting camps or other places where the floor creaks under his weight as he walks about. A word originally thought up by ASM3 Greg Quick.

Index

Sherman, Jim, 42, 158
Shooting at helicopters, Katrina, 146–147
Shop supervisor responsibilities, 94
Sikorsky H-52 Sea Guard, 4
Skarra, Dustin, 160
Sling deployment, 69, 86, 154–155
Smoke patterns, 120
Sprey, Zane, 35–36
Standardization team (Stan Team), 42–53
Structure, importance of, *44*
Sunset Limited train wreck, 54–57
Svensson, Daniel, 36

T

Teacher, role as, 105–108
Theodora fishing boat, 16–17
Thomas, Michael P., 32
Tisdale, Herb, 143–146
Torrens, Brad, 158
Training programs, establishing, 105–108
Train wreck, 54–57
Tropic Sun, 18
Tunks, Jeff, 42, 47–49

U

Urgent Marine Broadcast, 5, *18*
USS Jack Williams, 18
USS Seattle, 18

V

Ventilations, 46
Vertical-surface rescue technique, 104
Vogt, Anthony, 154

W

Wamble, Time, 154
Water rescue, first, 36–39

Waters, George, 94–98, 105
Watkins, Ed, 59
Watson, Jim, 99–104
Wet suits, 44–45
Whaley, Shawn, 97
Wilson, Gerry, 36

Y

Yates, Cole, 107
Yates, James Alan (Al), 66–81